Praise for

Laughing My Way

Through the Third Stage

"Susan Goldfein is funny. Very funny. If you are over sixty (and I am) and you need a laugh, a lift, or a better outlook on life (and I often need all three), read her book *Laughing My Way Through the Third Stage*. You'll be smiling all day long. In her early 70s, Susan found a new voice as a humorist in her amazing blog and newspaper column *Susan's Unfiltered Wit*. She is living proof that you're never too old to start something new."

—Andy Levine, Host, *Second Act Stories Podcast*

"Aging is not for sissies, but it isn't always serious either. So thank the stars that Susan's here to lighten things up! She writes what we've all thought about during this life stage and does it with wit, charm and wisdom. Universal themes layered with pure delight and topped with giggles...Susan serves up delectable treats for you to savor during your third act. Enjoy the feast that is this book!"

—Marcia Smalley, Life Coach, Writer, and Teacher

"Only Susan Goldfein can write about the 'joy' of getting older. Facing our golden years has never been so enjoyable as when Susan captures the spirit and fun all while we collect Social Security. Her collection of essays makes you forget about your aches and pains and replaces it with a never-ending smile on your face."

—Dan Roberts, Publisher/Editor, *The Vegas Voice*

PRAISE FOR *Laughing My Way Through the Third Stage*

"Having been born during WW II, I am a highly qualified old person. And I just want to say there's no one that tells my story quite like Susan Goldfein. Who would have thought that blurry vision and the prospect of losing your teeth could have a funny side? These treats and much more await you inside these covers. Buy this book!"

—Lucille K., Friend, Reader, and Paid Endorsement Writer

Laughing My Way Through the Third Stage

SELECTED ESSAYS THAT SKEWER THE GOLDEN YEARS

SUSAN GOLDFEIN

Copyright © 2022 by Susan Goldfein. All rights reserved. Printed in the United States of America. No part of this book may be used or reproduced in any manner whatsoever without written permission except in the case of brief quotations included in critical articles and reviews. For information, address Permissions@CitrinePublishing.com. The views expressed in this work are solely those of the author and do not necessarily reflect the views of the publisher.

The essays in this collection have previously appeared on the author's blog www.SusansUnfilteredWit.com.

Cover design and author photo by Mel Abfier

Library of Congress Cataloging-in-Publication Data

Goldfein, Susan
Laughing My Way Through the Third Stage:
Selected Essays that Skewer the Golden Years

p. cm.

Paperback ISBNs: 978-1-947708-59-4

Ebook ISBN: 978-1-947708-71-6

Library of Congress Control Number: 2022918352

10 9 8 7 6 5 4 3 2 1

First Edition, October 2022

 CITRINE PUBLISHING
State College, Pennsylvania, U.S.A.
(828) 585 - 7030
Publisher@CitrinePublishing.com
www.CitrinePublishing.com

For Larry, again and always

Contents

Contents

Introduction

"The older you get, I have to say, the funnier you find life. That's the only way to go. If you get serious about yourself as you get old, you are pathetic."

The quote above is from Diana Rigg, the actress, born 1938, died 2020. I found it in *The New York Times* on Monday, December 28, 2020, on a page that was a tribute to culture notables who died in 2020. Diana, I couldn't have said it better myself!

I, like many other vintage Americans, was introduced to Diana Rigg when she played Mrs. Emma Peele in the 1960s TV spy import from Britain, *The Avengers*. She was twenty-seven at the time. Younger fans remember her as the sharp-tongued Olenna from *Game of Thrones*. She was then seventy-five. In between is a long list of her other roles, from Shakespeare to James Bond.

If I'm correctly interpreting the intent of Dame Diana's statement, I believe she's saying that if one laments all the indignities of aging, there is a great risk of seeing oneself as a sad and pitiable creature. In other words, pathetic!

When I started my blog over ten years ago (that I have borrowed from for some of the essays in this book), the goal was to exercise my third-stage privilege of commenting on life with a bit of cynicism and satire. So, it was inevitable that as I moved further along the aging spectrum, I would turn that irony upon myself. After reading the words of Diana Rigg, I took stock of the occasions when I had actually made fodder out of my own condition.

I have questioned the wisdom of, at a certain age, paying a higher price for a product because it comes with a lifetime warranty. I applied the same logic before I chose to undergo some very expensive dental work. Did it come with a guarantee that I would outlive my teeth?

Skewering fashion and our changing body image is something that has brought me joy. The foolishness of trying to navigate a journey of a quarter mile wearing four-inch heels. The trauma of needing a new bathing suit. The question of whether going sleeveless was permissible after a certain age. Or creating a new publication, *The AARP Fall Fashion Preview,* after recognizing that, as an "older" woman, the glossy fashion magazines had nothing in them for me.

And talk about losses! And who, at this age, doesn't talk about losses? And losses come in many shapes and sizes. Unfortunately, there is the loss of friends, which is never funny. But what about the informal agenda of my husband's annual high school reunions? First, there is the rundown of the condition of one's body parts, then, who knows the best doctors, and finally, a drug update. All of which leads to the inevitable "alive or dead" game as they try to figure out if so-and-so, whom no one has heard from in quite a while, is simply ignoring the group or something worse.

I've written about losing my fingerprints, my left shoulder, the ability to sleep through the night, and losing almost two inches of height. Losing my cataracts was a welcome loss, but not without its downside. Seeing my face after the gauzy film was removed from my eyes made me want to consider cosmetic surgery as part of my aftercare.

And, of course, who could resist taking stabs at a society that tends to devalue us as we age. I say rail at those who judge us as dinosaurs because we still use AOL. And fie on the media who insists on describing anyone over sixty as "elderly." Or those who say "she used to be very pretty" about a woman of a certain age because she doesn't look like she did when she was sixteen.

There are more essays I could mention, but I think I've made my point about a shared philosophy. And so, dear Diana, it's too bad you never got to read my blog posts. You would have been very proud of me!

And let me end this with some wisdom from another celebrity icon, Betty White, who lived to nearly 100. In an interview on *Entertainment Tonight,* she said that she planned to spend her 100th birthday in quarantine due to Covid. Unfortunately, she didn't quite make it. And what did she say was the secret to a long life? Why, a sense of humor, of course.

Romancing the Crone

For those of you who have imagined me lounging by the pool during my retirement years, nothing could be further from the truth. In fact, I've been lounging on my screen porch, which is nowhere near the pool, and doesn't dictate that I wear a bathing suit. But I have not been idle.

As a matter of fact, I've been very busy pondering life, and how I might best find purpose for all those estrogen-free years that lay ahead. You see, I was a post-menopausal seeker, looking for role models for the next stage of life. I refused to accept that gray hair, a few wrinkles, and five extra pounds of tummy fat somehow reduced my societal net worth. (Although, I do admit it does give one pause!)

Although I've reached a point in life when my age exceeds the speed limit, I am not ready to step aside. Surely, I still had something to contribute.

I had heard of cultures which revered older women. And it was in this enlightened realm that I discovered the Triple Goddess—the representation of the three stages of a woman's life. The Triple Goddess! Where had she been all my life? I had blithely experienced Stage One, The Maiden, and Stage Two, The Mother, with a total lack of awareness of my inherent value. No way was I going to blow Stage Three!

The more I learned, the less I feared being discarded because I was an "older woman." True, there were certain things I could no longer do, like become a Victoria's Secret model. Not unless they added about six more inches of fabric to their panties, and two more cup sizes to their bra inventory.

But neither would I agree to be ignored or overlooked by a youth-worshipping society. I had discovered a place of honor. I would embrace Stage Three of the Goddess cycle and live out my remaining years as a Crone.

A Crone! I heard you gasp. But let me reassure you. Not the crone (not the small "c") as represented by the witch in "Hansel and Gretel," but the beautiful and benevolent Crone who appears as Cinderella's fairy godmother. The problem-solver who turns mice into horses and pumpkins into coaches. Okay, so I'm exaggerating. I don't really intend to mess around with plants and animals. But I will strive to become the authentic Crone—the honored third aspect of the Triple Goddess.

According to legend, the Crone is a symbol of self-value and respect. She is venerated for her experience, judgement, and wisdom—and clearly someone to turn to when you don't know the answer to Final *Jeopardy!*

To quote from one description of the Crone Goddess, she is "the wisdom keeper, seer, healer, and midwife, whose knowledge is sought out to guide others during life's hardships and transitions." Cool. Although I think I can do without the midwife part.

I hope it's not too late for me. With all this guiding and healing to accomplish, I probably should have started "Croning" years ago. But I'm a hard worker and have confidence that I can catch up.

I do have one question, though. Must I look the part? Does deciding to become a Crone require a new outfit? I'm sure Crones no longer wear gowns and tiaras or carry magic wands. But must I let my hair grow, and purchase flowing robes? Or will people take me just as seriously if I choose Not Your Daughter's Jeans and a T-shirt?

No matter. The important thing is to make up for lost time and immediately get to work on developing my wise-woman energy.

I'm really looking forward to engaging in my new role. Since I'm a novice, I will begin in the safe bosom of my very own family, and maybe work my way out to a few close friends. I'll have to let them know that I'm available for advice dispensing.

Do I wait for them to come to me, or do I take the first step? Should I tell my son that he should shave his beard immediately because it makes him look like a red-headed Smith Brother? Or tell my husband that the color of his favorite sports jacket gives him the appearance of someone with the flu?

I don't think so. Because a truly wise woman knows when to shut up.

To Do, or Not to Do, That is the Question

I just had another birthday. How do I feel about that? Since you only stop having them after you're dead, I guess I feel pretty good. In fact, I've recently made some serious investments in the future by electing to renew my car registration for two years instead of one, and my membership in AARP for another five. How's that for a burst of optimism?

As with each New Year, birthdays are a good time for reassessment. So, I begin with a physical inventory. All in all, I'm not doing too badly. My knees still bend and I'm able to navigate a staircase. My hips remain, as always, too wide, but the joints are articulating. My back? I'd rather not discuss it. Let's just say it's no worse. Only one new infirmity to complain about—the chronic pain in my left elbow. This has impacted my life by curtailing my golf game. Which is not necessarily a bad thing.

As I reflect, I'm reminded that six years ago this month, while engaged in my annual birthday retrospective, I had concluded that, going forward, I needed to master the art of relaxation. To accomplish this, my plan was to go outside with a kitchen timer and force myself to sit still and focus on reading material or simply daydream for incrementally increasing time periods. This was in lieu of my usual pattern, which was to pop out of my chair to pull a weed, water a plant, or pick up dog poop.

"How'd that work out for you?" you might ask. And even if you don't (ask, that is), I will share. For the past half-dozen years, my grass has been devoid of weeds, my flowers sufficiently hydrated, and you can safely walk barefoot over every inch of my property. Oh, and I've accumulated an impressive pile of back issues of *The New Yorker* magazine.

So, in February of 2020, I attempted to again tackle this issue with new insights. I have always prided myself on my stamina and ability to navigate through a hectic day, even though it's no longer necessary that I do so. I'm retired, the children have flown, there's a lot less laundry, and cooking dinner has become a quaint concept. Life could really slow down. If I let it.

But apparently, I have a bad case of OHDH syndrome. Don't bother looking for this disorder in the *Physician's Desk Reference* (or Dr. Google). You won't find it. I just made it up. So much of my adult life was spent as Wonder Woman, but without the skimpy outfit. Work, school, family, shopping, cooking, appointments, dates, dog, taking laundry out of the dryer at eleven at night. Living each day like a perpetual motion machine. I would walk into my apartment after a day of work and with my right hand, throw down my handbag, while my left hand retrieved the spaghetti pot. All accomplished in one smooth motion.

My personal feedback loop from all this hyperactivity was adjectives such as capable, energetic, tireless, maybe-just-a-little stressed, and youthful. It was a self-image I savored, one that is difficult to relinquish. Which leads to the current diagnosis: Old Habits Die Hard. Especially when it comes to one's identity.

But now, six years after the last attempt, perhaps it's time to try again for an image makeover. And I have a tiny piece of evidence that this time, I just might be on the right path.

A few days ago, as is my wont, I overbooked. My calendar indicated that I had committed to appointments back-to-back that seriously overlapped with Sam the Dog's dinner hour, and early evening walk. How could I let this happen? Silly question to ask of Wonder Woman.

In the manner to which I was accustomed, I began to strategize. If I left appointment #1 a few minutes earlier, and the traffic lights were with me, I could rush home, take care of Dog, maybe even refresh my eye liner, change into non-sensible shoes, jump back in the car, and if the lights were with me, be on time for appointment #2.

But rather than push forward into the race, I suddenly stopped in my tracks, took a deep breath, and said "No! I don't want to do this. I'm tired." I was able to cancel appointment #1, and so I did. Lying down on my bed for a bit of respite, I felt a sense of what could only be described as relief. This was okay. I have earned this right. I can act my age, whatever that means. I have nothing more to prove.

So, am I now on a new path that gives me permission to move over to the slower lane? I hope so. But to be sure, check back with me in six more years. How's that for another burst of optimism?

What's in It for Me?

Can you believe it's already mid-September? Where have all the flowers gone? The summer flew by as quickly as if it were being pursued by a pack of coyotes. Now, all the signs of fall are in the air—shorter days, cooler nights, and (according to my runny nose and itchy eyes), whichever pollen is released into the atmosphere after Labor Day.

And as much as some of us hate to see summer disappear, we are motivated to turn our attention to our wardrobes. Do we play by the old rules and pack away those whites until next Memorial Day, or abide by "white is still all right?"

And, who can resist the temptation of perusing the fall fashion supplements that arrive with our newspapers, or of browsing through a fashion magazine as we wait at the check-out line in the local supermarket?

One such opportunity presented itself to me as I sat in the waiting room of one of the many doctors I visit every September. (Fall also happens to be my check-up season.) Laying on the coffee table was the very hefty volume of the latest *Vogue* magazine, loudly announcing that it was "The September Issue" and inviting me to "Come On In." Anticipating the average forty-five-minute wait to see the doctor, I calculated that I probably had enough time to flip through at least half of the more than 592 pages. And so, I did. Went on in, that is.

And what was in it for me? Absolutely nothing! Unless I wanted to emulate some fourteen-year-old model in six-inch stilettos and a low-cut suit jacket with nothing underneath. Or consider a short skirt with boots rising to mid-thigh. Or how about a T-shirt sporting a picture of Alice Cooper?

Women of a certain age (and men, too) once again have been overlooked by the media and the fashion industry! Nowhere among those glossy pages was there a representation of the millions of us who are more concerned with fashionably concealing than revealing.

Still with time on my hands, I wondered what a fashion magazine would contain if it were geared toward the Medicare set. And who would publish it? Let me share with you some preliminary thoughts about my fantasy publication.

Welcome to the Latest Issue of The AARP Magazine Fall Fashion Preview

The Practical Stiletto

We are proud to feature the latest fashion in footwear for fall. Jimmy Choo's heretofore unknown half-brother, Seymour, has designed the perfect shoe for the fashion-conscious woman who is also concerned with avoiding hip replacement surgery. Meet the new stiletto—the one with the removable heel. Unlike his half-brother, Sy Choo really gets older women. The long thin heel is perfect for crossing a sexy leg while seated, or for quietly standing still while posing for a family photo. But want to walk from point A to point B? Simply unscrew the heels, tuck them discreetly into your purse, and voila! You are comfortably and safely on terra firma.

Retro Fit

Everything old is new again! The fashion house of Yves St. Laurent revives the trapeze shape! Those YSL folks understand that women of a certain age desire to look fashionable and trim, but also reject Spanx and other confining undergarments. Enter the trapeze dress. A big hit in the 50s, the line has been updated to suit the modern Medicare recipient who wants to be chic, and yet discrete about her muffin tops. Add a pair of low-heeled sensible shoes and you're ready for the fall season. Available in two slimming shades: black and ebony.

Not Your Daughter's Thongs

Feel foolish wearing bikini underwear? Tummy revealing those few extra pounds that came from who knows where? Don't despair. You can still feel sexy in today's high-waisted briefs! Every woman knows that the backbone of any good wardrobe is their undies (along with bras that actually fit). So, here's the skinny on the latest skivvies: for that woman of a certain age, we present the extra cut and coverage line of high-waisted underwear. These little cuties are far from frumpy. Made with lace in all the right places, they feature polka dots, stripes, and flashy patterns that you wouldn't be caught dead in wearing on the outside. But under those trapeze dresses, why not have a little bit of fun?

The Hot New Jumpsuit? Yes, You Can!

Good news! You don't have to avoid the versatile jumpsuit just because your last birthday came with more frequent trips to the loo. Thanks to Neiman-Marcus and the House of DVF, you can enjoy the long, lean look afforded by this sexy one-piece garment without the stress of removing it before you lose bladder control. Today's jumpsuit for the older woman comes with quick-release features that assure you will always look cool…and stay dry. So, whether you want one of these cuties for casual wear, or a black silk for a formal occasion, go for it! Be daring! Remember, relief is just a snap away.

To be continued, folks. The nurse just called my name. Please feel free to send me any ideas of your own. I'd be happy to forward them to AARP for their first fashion issue. So, be sure to look inside. It's all there for us!

Playing It Cool

(With special thanks to Allie, Chloe, and Jack)

I believe, by dint of diligence and a sassy haircut, that I have obtained Cool Grandparent status. I try to stay in touch with things that interest my iGen and post-iGen grandkids. Whether it's the latest music and who's #1 on the charts (do they still have charts?), or the current iconic sports figure, I try to be "woke."

I'm on top of the latest meme and try never to throw shade, at least not where they can hear me. I don't yet have a tattoo, but I'm considering it, as well as an additional piercing—somewhere.

But if one wants to retain one's Cool Grandparent certificate, one can never rest on one's chocolate chip cookies. No. Hipness takes work and continuing education credits.

So, at dinner the other night, when I heard my three youngest grandkids animatedly discussing their latest passion, my ears, still with only one piercing on each lobe, naturally perked up. The subject of their excitement, I soon discovered, was a video game called *Fortnite*, which, apparently, they had been playing all summer. *OMG*, I texted to my brain, *how did I miss this?* My status was in jeopardy, and I had to act quickly. I accepted the challenge and asked them if they would make the time to teach me to play. They said they would check their calendars and get back to me.

Let me state at the outset that I have zero experience with video games. Unless you count the wasted hours of my youth playing pinball. I was already an adult during the golden age of Space Wars, Pac Man, and Pong, and while I was aware of their existence and popularity, I wasn't quite ready for a second childhood. When we dropped off our own kids at video arcades, I never considered staying to play.

But I was confident when said grandkids finally made room on their schedules and got back to me with an appointment. *I can do this*, I thought. Unlike some other body parts stiffened by arthritis, I believed my thumbs to be in good working order. And, as part of my ongoing struggle to leave the Mesozoic era, I do embrace technology. To some extent.

So, on a chilly late afternoon, I found myself on a large sofa in the family playroom, surrounded by three tutors who at least seemed excited to be teaching Grandma how to play *Fortnite*.

Inquiring minds want to know. Thus, the session began with me asking dumb questions, which they patiently answered. For example, why was the game called *Fortnite*? (I omitted Part II of the question, which was, why was it incorrectly spelled?) I was informed that one of the original playing objectives was to remain alive for two weeks. However, for their version, it was last man standing. Either way, I got the message that the theme was not about brotherly love.

14

My youngest tutor grabbed the controls and powered up. I was treated to an intricate graphic display, as the wall-sized TV screen lit up to reveal a dystopian setting, which, shall we say, was not exactly Disneyland. Danger was looming everywhere!

The first thing I was required to do was choose a character, or a "skin" to be my avatar. *"Sweet,"* I thought, *"maybe I could find some sexy representation of my real self, one maybe ten pounds thinner."* But since I wasn't an official card-carrying, V-bucks-wealthy member of the *Fortnite* community, I couldn't purchase my own skin. So, my grandson graciously let me borrow his. My skin, therefore, was male, or at least I believe he was. I think he's best described as the result of a one-off between the Incredible Hulk and an armadillo. Not quite what I had in mind.

I was handed the game controller and shown the functions of the various buttons that would allow me to navigate the violence and determine my survival as I proceeded to kill the zombies. My skin was dropped from the sky, not with a parachute, but holding an umbrella decorated with a menacing-looking spider's web. Imagine Mary Poppins on testosterone and maybe you can get the picture.

As I landed atop a structure that was reminiscent of a gallows, my Mary Poppins accessory turned into a pickaxe, and I was ready to attack. My capable thumbs flew into action as I moved my character forward, backward, sideways to escape the threatening hordes of the undead. Peril was everywhere and tension was mounting. At various times, my pickaxe morphed into a sword, then a machine gun, or whatever else was necessary for my defense. And all this action was occurring as storms were brewing, which were also a threat to my on-line existence. It was all quite breathtaking and might have necessitated an additional blood pressure pill!

There are many more variables in this highly nuanced game of survival, but hey, this was just my first lesson. I'm proud to say I did manage to destroy my share of zombies. But alas, no doubt due to my underdeveloped visuomotor coordination, I was finally taken down.

I came away from my tutorial wondering about the violence in which I had just participated. I asked my grandkids how they thought this impacted them and was assured that they accept it as pure fantasy. And I remembered that the cartoons I used to watch, where characters got their heads bashed in or were flattened by steam rollers, did not turn me into a serial killer.

So, how did I score on my first attempt at online gaming? I placed 46th out of 100 players. My grandkids thought this was pretty good. And so, I left the game room, relieved that my Cool Grandma status was no longer in jeopardy. Perhaps they will even grant me an appointment for a second lesson in the not-too-distant future.

Taken Without a Grain of Salt

It seems to me there's a critical age at which, each time you add another candle to your cake, you also add another health care practitioner. If I reviewed my count of medical specialists, let's say, at age thirty-five, the list might just fit on the head of a pin. And now, I believe I'd need to inscribe said list on something at least as large as a family-sized pizza!

What brings this to the forefront at this particular time is not my own cadre of doctors, but my husband's. His personal list now includes a brand new "ologist," an otherwise lovely man who has further complicated our lives. In the interest of longevity, we already practice a low-fat, low-carb, low-gluten, Paleo, Mediterranean, don't-eat-white-foods lifestyle. Mostly. With some exceptions. But if we wanted to enjoy even more time "on golden pond," this new doc on the block strongly recommended that my husband significantly reduce his salt intake.

Eliminating salt from one's diet may not sound like a big deal. It's seemingly simple. When eating your scrambled eggs whites, don't pick up the saltshaker. Or order a side of bacon. Ever. Or make pancakes from one's favorite healthy pancake mix because the salt content is enough to keep you afloat even if you can't swim.

While salt has not been restricted from my diet, at least not yet, what else can a supportive wife do but join her husband on his low-sodium journey?

Step One was to search the pantry and refrigerator for offending foods. Out went the ketchup (organic), the soy sauce, the crackers, and the can of mixed nuts. Even something as benign as cottage cheese was now a potential killer. Ever read the sodium content on packaged bread items? Positively terrifying! Life, moving forward, would definitely be a challenge.

Step Two was a trip to the supermarket to begin the reeducation process. Reading glasses in hand, I pushed my cart up and down the aisles, lifting jars, bottles, cans, and loaves, reading the fine print, and trying to replace my discarded groceries with sodium-free or low-sodium substitutes. I was heavily into condiments when my cell phone rang. It was my husband reminding me that I had been gone for almost three hours. I assured him I'd be home as soon as I finished researching the dairy aisle.

The new reality was that more home cooking was in order. And I certainly don't mind cooking up a pot of pasta sauce or soup from scratch. Or sprinkling a salad with home-made dressing, sans salt. But baking my own bread? Sorry, but my pioneer instincts stretch only so far.

Therefore, Step Three of the new program was a search for a salt-free bread that came wrapped in plastic and sealed with a twist tie. Success was achieved at my local health food store. There, I discovered, in the back of a freezer, a loaf of sliced bread that promised to be my alternative to an acquaintance with yeast. I gasped at the price tag, but, hey, what's a few extra dollars where health is concerned? This baby was coming home with me.

Anxious to sample a piece before I introduced it to my husband, I removed a frozen slice and placed it in the toaster. When it was sufficiently warm, I took my first bite.

Have you ever considered smearing butter and jam on the cardboard shipping box containing your latest Amazon delivery? I guarantee you that it couldn't taste much worse than what I was attempting to swallow. The rest of the loaf was immediately discarded, along with the dollars I had just spent. Clearly, my search for a healthy, leavened substitute was not over.

Eating at home is one thing when your diet is restricted but dining in a restaurant is quite another. And for better or worse, recreational eating has become a major part of our social life. This is particularly true during the winter months, when life in Florida involves reuniting with friends we haven't seen in nearly half a year, over dinner.

Now, added to the requirements for an acceptable restaurant, i.e., location, chair comfort, noise level lower than a subway station, air temperature that does not require a fur jacket, is—will the chef agree to cook your food without salt? The last thing you want when you're out for a pleasant evening is the wrath of the person in the toque because you requested that he or she put the sauce on the side.

So, gradually, we are adjusting. I'm becoming a very discerning label-reader, with a newly acquired recognition that sodium-free, low-sodium, reduced-sodium, and light sodium, don't all mean the same thing. I'm actually beginning to enjoy salt-less peanut butter, and the memory of that awful bread is slowly fading. Fortunately, I did locate an acceptable substitute, a mere forty-five-minute drive from our home!

And it's working. My husband is experiencing positive effects from our new, healthier, though somewhat blander, diet. And the lease *"on golden pond"* might just be renewed for a few additional (gulp!), salt-free years.

Is Your Email Address Telling on You?

Are you reluctant to share your age? Are you reluctant to share your email address? If you answered "yes" to the first question, and "no" to the second, and are an AOL user, you're screwed!

According to the popular wisdom proffered by millennials and beyond, if AOL appears after the @, you are fat, over eighty, a technology dinosaur, live in the suburbs, and probably have bad breath. (I didn't actually read about the last one; I just threw it in.) Furthermore, those brats claim that AOL users are clinging to an antique, are stuck in the 90s, and should never be taken seriously. About anything. Because we are blithering idiots.

And if you're looking for a job, don't dare indicate on your resume that AOL is your email account or you'll never get your foot in the door. Which isn't very relevant anyway if, in fact, you're over eighty, and applying to work at Home Depot.

Back in the day, if you wanted an email account and the ability to access the internet, America OnLine (It became AOL in 1991.) was the major player. Their disk packages were everywhere, free for the taking. So, we took. It was easy to set up an account, and soon the little yellow man was running across the computer screen, assuring you that your dial-up was working.

That's when I began using AOL. I did have a free Hotmail account for a while, but at the time, true to its name, it flooded my inbox with enticing ads for penile implants, pills that would enhance my sexual prowess, ways to meet hot babes, and phone numbers to call if I was interested in a three-way, in any combination of my choice. Eventually Hotmail left me cold.

Despite the fact that AOL-email shaming is rampant, I refuse to be intimidated. So, to people who say, "Why do you still use AOL?" I say, "Why not?" If something has been working for you for twenty years, why give it up? Why go through the trouble of changing, which involves contacting and updating every single person and entity that you know or have been doing business with for two decades? AOL has good security, adequate storage, spam protection, I like the interface, and I can access mail on all my other devices. Do I really need more? If someone invents an email account that vacuums the rug and washes windows, I might consider switching.

So what if I'm accused of being stuck in the 90s? What was so bad about the 90s and so good now? Some wonderful things happened in the 90s. Like the debut of the original *Law and Order* on TV. *Seinfeld* was hot and so was *The Sopranos*. It was the heyday of Tiger Woods and Michael Jordan. Bill Clinton redefined having sex, and boom boxes were replaced by the Walkman. (Okay, so we also had Celine Dion, Beanie Babies, and the Macarena, but you can't have everything.) And best of all, the world did not come to an end with Y2K.

And yes, I am very much aware that cooler alternatives to AOL do exist, like the very popular Gmail. But I find Google so pushy. They always want to know where I am and are constantly offering to store my passwords. Frankly, I think they're up to something. And what makes Google so cool anyway? Big deal that everyone shows up for work wearing T-shirts.

And then there's Yahoo. But do I really want an email address that has the resonance of a drunken cowboy slapping his horse? Therefore, for now, I will stand up to the derision, keep my AOL, and will continue to take comfort from that disembodied, but very familiar, voice informing me that I've got mail.

But, I can foresee a time in the future, perhaps when I go to meet my maker, that I may finally have to switch. Because in heaven, the only choice could very well be the Cloud.

The Grandma's Guide to Gorgeous

It has recently come to my attention that my fashion image is in serious need of a makeover. My entire wardrobe, which I believed to be tasteful and age-appropriate, is, in fact, quite boring. And boring is not the look for which I was striving.

This dismaying, and no doubt costly, epiphany dawned via a newspaper article featuring women ranging in age from sixty to ninety-four who, based on eyewear that occupied three-quarters of their faces, appeared to be kindred spirits of Iris Apfel. Their unique sense of style has made them internet stars, thereby anointing them as the new fashion influence for the Medicare set. So, move over, Brooks Brothers, and make way for the babes with the grandma faces!

All of the women in said article, when not rummaging in consignment shops for gently used Comme des Garçons, or Goodwill racks for someone's granddaughter's frayed jeans, are also bloggers. Well, I blog too, don't I? So, what's holding me back from being a geriatric sensation?

Tempted, but also timid, I launched an in-depth study of what it was that made these women so notable. I needed some fashion confidence if I was to join the ranks of the senior "slayers" and become an Instagram icon.

After reading the blogs and scrutinizing the photos, I think I've finally figured it out. Below, I offer the fruits of my labor—a list of helpful hints for becoming an audacious, subversive, riveting, cool, and attention-grabbing granny!

- Abandon most of your basic blacks, whites, and grays and replace them with wild, colorful prints and things that don't match.
- Forego modesty and don't be afraid to reveal body parts that may not have seen the light of day for decades.
- Gray hair is acceptable but cut it really short. Cropped bangs and shaved sides are uber cool. Wear it long and let it go completely wild or pile it like a bird's nest on top of your head. A purple streak gets you bonus points.
- Stash your demure button earrings and studs in the back of the jewelry drawer and rush out to purchase hoops— the bigger the better. If you can find a pair that looks like it could double as a perch for a parakeet, you're solid. And for a change of pace, switch off to a long dangling style. More bonus points if you have a pair that gives the impression of being plucked from Carmen Miranda's hat.
- Wear plenty of wide bracelets. On both wrists. Ones made from recycled African baobab trees are best. What's so special about baobab trees? Who knows? But if the bracelets weigh enough, they're also useful for bicep curls.

- If you sport a necklace, consider multiples, and make sure they're really chunky. They also serve to ward off unwanted hugs.
- Start to acquire a hat collection. The sillier the better. Turbans and baseball caps are acceptable, as are knitted pussy hats.
- Even if your vision is perfect, one or two pairs of eyeglasses the size of headlights from a Mack truck are a must. Black frames are best, but bright red with matching lipstick is also guaranteed to turn some heads.
- Accessorize your plain street clothes, i.e., T-shirt and sweats, with a touch of color. A pair of elbow-length gloves in fuchsia just might do the trick.
- Naked fingers are a definite a no-no. Flaunt multiple rings with large stones. They're also a handy self-defense weapon in case of a mugging. Blood-red nail polish puts the otherwise-ordinary hand over the top!
- Sport torn denim and T-shirts with messages, the raunchier the better. A white T with "Be A Slut" written in chartreuse cursive script is a guaranteed eye-catcher.
- Top off your mismatched outfit with an oversized cape. Add a mask and it doubles as a Zorro disguise for your next costume ball.
- Going out to dinner? How about an evening gown with high-top sneakers?

I'm well aware that the transformation from ordinary to extraordinary will not be easy, but some things are simply worth the effort. And I hope this guide will be helpful. So, please join me at the thrift shop. Why "go gentle into that good night" when all it takes is the perfect vintage handbag? Preferably in shocking orange.

Driver's Ed

There has been an amendment to my marriage contract. I'm not referring to a legal document that was signed in the presence of a lawyer or a rabbi, but an informal set of conventions that have evolved over time in the partnership.

Every marriage has one. It usually includes a tacit or explicit division of responsibilities that permits the union to function more-or-less efficiently on a daily basis. For example, in my marriage, I'm in charge of such details as making sure we don't run out of toilet paper, seeing to it that the dog is fed twice daily, changing light bulbs, and brewing coffee in the morning. My husband is in charge of the remote control.

And for most of our time together, he has been the family driver. Until recently. I am thankful to say that the change did not come about due to an illness or a serious incapacity. But rather, it began as a practical matter having to do with whose eyesight was better after dark. Mine.

While I'm sure there was some reluctance to relinquish control of the steering wheel, it had to be done. And there were definitely benefits to assuage the male ego, benefits like, perhaps, a little more wine with dinner? And a catnap on the way home from the movies?

The perks of being a passenger obviously did not go unnoticed, for soon there were seemingly innocent requests to be chauffeured in full sunlight. Usually something like, "Could you drive? I have to make a few calls," as he reaches into his pocket for the iPhone.

Let me state that I have no objection to change. Change can be healthy. It can signify that, like the Constitution, or your Facebook page, the marriage contract is a living document, capable of adapting to the needs of the present day. And I don't mind driving. It's the driving lessons I can do without!

We are about to set out to visit some friends on a Saturday afternoon.

"You drive," he says, "I have to return some emails." Out comes the iPhone as I slip into the driver's seat.

"Why are you backing out of the garage like that?" he asks.

"Like what?" I reply.

"You're turning the steering wheel twice, when I only have to turn it once."

"So? Did I hit anything?" He returns to his emails as I successfully pull out of our driveway. I apply the brakes as we come to a red light.

"You waited too long. You're going to ruin the brake linings."

"I have been driving since 1959 and all my brakes linings have always been pristine," I remind him.

"Well, it's dangerous to wait so long. You can hit the guy in front of you."

I also remind him that the only person in the car to have recently caused a fender-bender was him. Time to make another phone call.

"Why are you staying in this lane?" he asks as he finally notices that we have entered the highway. "All the other lanes are moving faster."

"Do you not see the fourteen-wheeler barreling down on my left?" I ask. "If I pull out now, we're going to ruin a lot more than the brake linings."

"Well, get out of this lane as soon as you can. You know I can't stand driving in slow traffic."

"Yes," I hiss through clenched teeth, "but you're not driving. Isn't there someone you need to text?"

We arrive at our friends' house without further comment, and I assume the driving lesson has ended. I head towards a parking space.

"Park there," he says, his finger wagging at a different spot.

"Why?" I ask.

"It's better."

In spite of the fact that I was contemplating divorce, we had a cheery afternoon, and then dinner at a lovely restaurant.

"How's the wine?" I ask him as I'm sipping my club soda.

"Quite good," he answers.

"So have a little more," I encourage.

Five minutes into the return trip, my darling falls asleep. Anticipating a peaceful ride home, I pray that he does not begin to snore. I'm lucky this time. I ride in blessed silence. I breathe a sigh of relief as I pull the car into our garage when, suddenly, Lazarus beside me strongly recommends that I back out and try it again.

Only this time, I should turn the wheel "more to the right" to so that when he backs out in the morning, he won't knock off the side-view mirror like he did last time when it was all my fault because I didn't park correctly.

And so, the journey ends as it began.

Looking ahead, I can see that this new arrangement in our marriage is going to be a challenge. There is nothing worse than a back-seat driver who is sitting right next to you. I wonder if there's a penalty for forcing your passenger to ride in the trunk. Whatever it is, it may be worth it. It has to be a lesser offense than murder.

The Eye of the Beholder

Has this ever happened to you?

You're in a restaurant. In your line of vision is another table with, let's say, three couples. You unconsciously absorb the physical details of the six well-dressed people who are about to eat their appetizers. You notice the gray hair on the partially bald men, the obviously chemically treated hair of the women, the flashlights on the iPhones to help illuminate the menu when reading glasses aren't enough. And yes, those are hearing aids snugly tucked behind at least three pairs of ears. And your conclusion? Boy, there's sure a lot of old people in this place!

Sticking with reality for the moment, as painful as that might be, the fly on the wall tells you that the woman on the left is celebrating her birthday tonight. And guess what? She is, in fact, a whole year younger than you are. Wow, she should take better care of herself!

The question is, how accurately do we see ourselves? In public places, I frequently find myself scrutinizing people I consider "older," trying to determine their ages. Funny how I consistently conclude that they must be at least ten years older than I am.

With each passing year, reconciling my chronological age with the "me" that exists inside my head, is becoming more and more challenging. The person that lives behind my face cannot possibly be related to that DOB I just wrote down on the doctor's intake form!

While I can't exactly pinpoint at precisely which decade my self-view became arrested, I can assure you that my alter ego is, in fact, still paying full price for a movie ticket. And that lovely twenty-one-year-old woman calling for "Grandma" can't possibly mean me. Contrary to what you might be thinking, I don't avoid mirrors. That would be difficult, if not impossible. I prefer to confront my reflection rather than poke myself in the eye with a mascara wand.

But I have discovered a few enhancement tricks that I'm happy to share. Be sure to place your mirror away from the possibility of naked sunlight streaming through the window. And never, never make the mistake of looking into a magnified make-up mirror while wearing a pair of reading glasses!

And what about photographs? I will admit that lately I've grown more camera-shy. The person living inside my head is not always happy to be mistaken for the woman in the picture. And selfies are definitely a no-no. My arms aren't long enough.

I know that men can have a similar reaction. My husband, for example, is frequently alarmed by his captured image, and can be heard to mutter, "Who's that old man?"

And then there's my ninety-one-year-old uncle who stated the other day that his peers "look so old," implying with that comment that he didn't see himself that way. He might be correct. I don't know his friends.

So, do I really want to know how the rest of the world views me, or continue to exist in the bubble labeled "you're as young as you feel?" And except for the forty-five minutes in the morning that it takes me to recover from night-time stiffness, fortunately, I feel pretty good.

But the illusion is not foolproof. In spite of my personal inner life, the world continually presents a series of reality checks. The cashier behind the ticket window never asks me for proof of age when I say, "one senior, please." (Well, what can you expect? She's probably only eighteen and everyone over thirty looks old to her!)

Young men have occasionally offered me a seat on a crowded bus. I don't require it, but I accept. Pride is one thing, comfort quite another. The bagger in the supermarket offers to help me load my cart full of groceries into my car. I flex my muscles and tell him, "I'll be fine, thank you." Clearly, he has no clue that he is addressing a much younger woman than may appear in his mirror.

Despite considering myself to be a confident woman with real, more serious values, I have a sneaky feeling that this duel between perception and reality will go on. And I will continue to derive pleasure and satisfaction from hearing (from someone who has just learned my age), "Oh, I'm shocked. You certainly don't look it!" Not like those other guys. You know, the ones in the restaurant.

It could very well be that this phenomenon is just a normal part of the aging process. (Not that I'm aging, of course.)

And perhaps this quote says it all: "Inside every older person there's a younger person wondering what happened!"

The Meaning of Life (Time Warranty)

Come on, admit it. We're all subject to occasional morbid thoughts, especially at that point in life when the number representing our chronological age exceeds the highway speed limit. Don't tell me that you never think about the Grim Reaper, the Dark Angel, or any of the other euphemisms you can name to avoid the "D" word.

I confess to having morbid thoughts on three different occasions during the past month.

Maybe it was prophetic, but what most recently got me thinking about time and mortality was the need for a new watch. An awkward movement of my left elbow while leaning in to apply mascara had landed my old, faithful, *expensive* timepiece on the unforgiving tile floor of the bathroom. Its poor little face was smashed to smithereens, and even with my untrained eye, I knew it was broken beyond repair.

The next day, I called upon my friend, the consummate shopper (every woman knows one), who, of course, directed me to the *absolute best* place to purchase a new watch. As I perused the jewelry case, looking for watches whose numbers could be seen without the aid of reading glasses, I was approached by a salesman who offered to help. He removed several models from the case and laid them before me on the requisite piece of black velvet cloth.

He pointed out the virtues of each model, stopping at one that he declared to be a little more expensive, but came with a life-time warranty. His comment was the catalyst for Morbid Thought #1. *Whose lifetime*, I mused, *mine or the watch's?*

At that precise moment, I happened to glance at another customer who was at least thirty years my junior. Pointing in her direction, I asked the salesman, "See that woman over there? If she buys this watch, does she also get a lifetime warranty?"

"She certainly does," he replied as if talking to someone recently declared incompetent.

"Then I should get a discount, shouldn't I?"

"A discount?" he repeated, with an unnecessarily steep rising inflection.

"Of course," I answered in my best 'isn't-it-obvious' tone of voice. "She is clearly a good deal younger than I. Therefore, her lifetime warranty will be in effect much longer than mine, so why should I be charged the same?"

He opened his mouth to speak, but said nothing. I left him to ponder my logic, and decided not to purchase a new watch that day.

Morbid Thought #2, by sheer coincidence, also occurred during a shopping trip, interrupting an otherwise very pleasant afternoon. This time, I was accompanying my husband, who was on a quest to find the perfect sweater. We were in the men's department of a fine store, and since I knew what he liked, we separated to cover more territory in less time. I wasn't successful, but when I rejoined him, he had found two potential candidates.

Both sweaters were the same style, both flattering colors, both a fine wool. One, however, was significantly more expensive than the other, and therein was the dilemma. Rationalizing the possible expenditure of some extra dollars, he stated that the sweater that cost more would probably last longer.

That's when it happened. I thought, but didn't dare utter, *at our age, can you be sure you'll get your money's worth?*

He must have read my mind, because in the next instant we were walking to the checkout counter with the black cashmere V-neck sporting the lower price tag.

Morbid Thought #3, which was, in reality, a morbid utterance, snuck up on me during the performance of a very ordinary domestic task—replacing a missing button on my husband's shirt. My hand stopped in mid-air as I thought of other small, "maternal" functions I had assumed over the years, such as re-threading the drawstring which, for some reason he was forever dislodging from his sweatpants.

"Honey," I called to him. He responded on my third attempt to get his attention.

"Yes?" he said, as he raised his head from his iPhone.

"I was just thinking," I said, as I lifted the shirt towards him, "in the event that I should pass on before you, would you like me to teach you how to do this?"

He laughed heartily, though I'm not sure at what.

I'm pleased to say that I haven't had another morbid thought in at least a week. Maybe this is predictive of a trend. I hope so. I am, in fact, feeling so optimistic that I went watch shopping again, but to an altogether different store.

The friendly salesman spread out the black velvet cloth, upon which he placed three different models, all fashionable, all with numbers that could be easily read without intense magnification.

"And this one," he said, lifting one of the watches off the cloth, "costs just a little more than the other two, but comes with a twenty-five year warranty."

"Great," I said. "I'll take it."

Outliving My Teeth

I had an experience recently, which was an eye-opener. Or I should say mouth-opener because it concerned a visit to the dentist.

While dental visits are not on my list of top-ten earthly delights, it was the only way I could think of to get a chronically loose crown reaffixed. All I had at my disposal was Elmer's Glue, which is for external use only. And I make it a policy never to tamper with warning labels.

"Well," Dr. Painless said, "I don't know how long we can keep doing this. You really ought to consider an implant. Or two." He said this as casually as if he were suggesting I purchase a scoop of ice cream, or two, and not something that was going to require a root canal. "And by the way," he added, "when was the last time you had a full set of X-rays?"

Gee, I hadn't exactly entered that information into my diary, so I looked at him dumbly and said, "I really don't know." That was the wrong answer. I should have invented some specific time frame. My failure to do so resulted in consigning my mouth to withstand the pain and suffering of having to bite down on at least a dozen pieces of film framed in cardboard stiff enough to support the roof of a small building.

The target number of X-rays was sixteen, but I informed the clinician after I had endured the first twelve, that there would be no more. I spewed this out with my jaws clenched, lest she try to sneak another one in there if I opened my mouth to speak.

Very proud of myself for resisting, I sat in the dental chair, enjoying the relief from no longer having sharp edges digging into my palate. That is, until the dentist reentered, put the developed pictures on the light box, and turned to me with a facial expression that could not have been more serious than if he was about to announce my imminent demise. Instead, he focused my attention on the light box, upon which were my illuminated teeth, roots and all, in various shades of black and white.

I don't know about you, but I find looking at dental X-rays a real turnoff. In general, I prefer to remain unacquainted with non-visible body parts. (In fact, now that I have gotten older, I find I would rather ignore even some visible body parts.) Once, a doctor sent me full-color photographs showing the results of my latest colonoscopy. Perhaps if I didn't know what I was looking at I might have found it more aesthetically pleasing, but I doubt it. I mean really, a nice letter telling me that everything was fine would have sufficed.

So, as I stare at the skeletal images that look like something out of a horror movie, Dr. P is explaining, with the aid of a laser pointer and a professorial voice, that while my teeth are fine, my inner bones are in a tragic state. If I don't act immediately, I am at risk for becoming edentulous. Several sentences later I finally figure out that "edentulous" means that one day I shall be toothless! Well, won't we all, if we live long enough?

He goes on to suggest an emergency appointment with a specialist. I was to leave the realm of the dentist and enter the rarified world of the "dontist." (It was to be my first "dontol" experience, having been spared the need for an orthodontist when I was a child.)

Dutifully, I now sit in the plush examination chair in the plush office of the periodontist, listening to him "tsk" and "hmm" as he reviews my X-rays. I am getting a sinking feeling that I am about to be asked to contribute financially to these fine surroundings and the half-dozen lovely female assistants moving to and fro. He does not disappoint.

The treatment he is suggesting to prevent further destruction of that which is holding my teeth in place, plus two dental implants, comes with a hefty price tag. This is way more than the Required Minimum Distribution from my IRA!

I need some time to think this over. "Can you give me a minute alone with my X-rays?" I implore the good doctor. He complies, says he understands, and will come back in five minutes.

My mind races through various pathetic scenarios: how much longer do I have before my molar gets stuck in a piece of toasted bagel, my incisor cracks while biting a crisp, juicy apple, or kernels of corn are being scraped off the cob because I can no longer safely gnaw? Wait! I think I just hit on the heart of the matter! Maybe it is a matter of time!

The "dontist" returns and asks me if I have reached a decision. In the tradition of my ancestors, I respond to his question with a question of my own. "So, tell me, doctor, how long do I have?" He looks perplexed. "Before my teeth fall out," I reply. "Five years, ten years?" He says he can't tell me that with any accuracy. He is reluctant to give me even a ballpark.

"Why do you ask?" he queries. I fire another question. "Do you know how old I am?" He looks at my chart, and answers "yes," he has that information. "So," I reason, "if my teeth will last another ten years without this expensive treatment, perhaps that is good enough. And if I agree to this expensive treatment, can you give me a guarantee of longevity?"

I knew immediately that he thought I was being highly unreasonable. And, of course, I was. But I think there comes a time in one's life when it is not inappropriate to measure the risks, discomfort, and costs of one's non-life-threatening condition, against the risks, discomfort and costs of treating the non-life-threatening condition.

In the end, I agree to the dental work. And I believe it will be worth it. Because now, in addition to the hope that one day my bachelor sons will decide to marry, outlasting my teeth has given me something else to live for!

Steppin' Out with My Baby

I have mixed feelings about formal occasions. On the one hand, each one is an opportunity to release my inner child and play dress-up. On the other hand, my outer "mature" adult cringes as it contemplates the possible necessity of Spanx or other constricting undergarments. Even the idea of panty hose makes me shudder.

So, when the invitation came, requesting our attendance at a charity ball as the guests of the honoree, my inclination was to say, "No. Thank you very much for asking," and send a donation. My life would be no less rich for having missed one more mass-produced meal and some boring speeches. And I could lounge comfortably at home in my finest Russell athletic wear, sans undergarments if I so chose.

But there was a personal connection to the guest of honor, so we accepted. Besides, the venue was enticing. The affair was to be held on the *USS Intrepid*, the WWII aircraft carrier that is now a sea, air, and space museum located on Manhattan's west side. Even if it did not turn out to be entertaining, the evening at least held the prospect of being educational.

A formal event such as the one I'm describing, I believe, brings to light yet another significant difference between the sexes. I highly doubt that a man is challenged by the phrase "formal attire." He simply reaches into the closet, unzips the protective garment bag, removes the tuxedo, and hopes that it still fits. Then, because errand running is encoded into female DNA, he simply must hope that this wife remembered to pick up his pleated shirt from the cleaners after it was last worn.

But a woman, no matter how extensive her wardrobe, will arrive at the inevitable conclusion that she has nothing to wear, despite the perfectly good little black numbers already hanging in her closet. Hence, she must shop for the perfect dress.

This shopping excursion is no mere lark, however. For women of a certain age, it can be a devastating experience. Second only to trying on bathing suits.

Unlike men, who have only to don the equivalent of a school uniform, women are faced with endless choices when it comes to formal attire. Arriving at the best decision requires careful consideration and a frank confrontation with one's anatomy. Which body parts can be revealed, and which are best left undercover?

Personally, I believe I've surpassed the upper limit on strapless. But there remains the issue of cleavage. What about sleeve length? (Be honest: do the upper arms jiggle more than they did last year?) And hemline…how much leg do I dare show?

After an agonizing, self-critical afternoon, I purchase yet another short, black, sleeveless cocktail dress. Thankfully, it is not clingy and will require no masochistic undergarments. I have thoughtfully concluded that my knees and upper arms can handle the exposure. I decide to ignore the issue of elbows. I can't see them, anyway.

The day of the event, I am gathering my accessories and discover to my horror that I do not own a pair of dressy black shoes. How have I existed without this essential? Clearly, I have to get out more.

I make an emergency trip to a local shoe store. There, I find myself gazing at, not footwear, but weapons! Six-inch stiletto heels attached to a sole and some straps that look like evil props from a James Bond movie. But I know that the only person I would kill with those heels is myself.

"Don't you have a dressy black shoe with a lower heel?" I pathetically ask the clerk. She's smiling, but I know she's thinking I should try the orthopedic store around the corner. Nevertheless, she wants to be helpful—or at least make her commission—so she disappears into the mysterious back room where shoe salespeople seem to disappear for all eternity, and finally emerges with two shoe boxes.

She removes the box covers to reveal a pair of silver sandals and a pair of elegant black pumps. I'm drawn to the elegant black pumps and am pleased to note they don't have six-inch heels. By comparison, the four-inch heels don't seem that high. In retrospect, I realize that my perception of reality had been seriously altered.

I try on the shoes as cautiously as if they were glass slippers. They're a good fit and hug my foot comfortably. So far, so good. But I have yet to stand up.

Slowly and carefully, I rise, hoping that my Medicare card is tucked safely in my wallet. The sensation is vaguely reminiscent of wearing ice skates for the first time and I suddenly want to grab onto a railing. Like a cautious toddler, I take my first step, then another. *Not bad. I can do this.* I'm pleased as I catch a glimpse of my legs in the mirror. Very sexy. Sold!

From the moment I stepped out of the taxi that evening, I knew I had made a terrible mistake. I was yet another victim of fashion. I was afraid to move. I was trapped and terrified. For some reason, strutting around the shoe store and walking on actual pavement were two entirely different experiences. Out in the real world, my mobility had been seriously compromised.

Women all around me seemed to be moving with no difficulty on heels even higher than mine. If they could walk without fearing for their lives, why couldn't I? So what if some of them were thirty years younger? I had more experience. I had been walking longer.

I decided there must be a balancing technique that they knew, and I didn't. So, I experimented with various postural adjustments. Holding my shoulders back and thrusting my pelvis forward allowed me at least enough momentum to catch up with my husband, who, bless his heart, seemed unaware that I was no longer at his side.

I immediately linked my arm in his and told him that the only time he could leave me for even one second was when I was safely in a chair.

Did I mention that we were on an aircraft carrier? Of course, when I chose those shoes, I never considered that we would be navigating the length of three football fields to reach the dining hall. Clinging to my husband, it was indeed the longest trek of my life. I felt as challenged as the man who walked a tightrope across the Grand Canyon. In fact, at that moment, I would have happily traded places with him.

I did not leave my seat once for the entire evening. Dancing was out of the question. As was a seriously needed trip to the ladies' room. I have no idea what we were served for dinner, because I was completely preoccupied with the notion that at the end of the evening, I would have to walk all the way back.

Eventually, the night was over. We thanked our host and I lied as I told him what a lovely evening it had been. After all, it wasn't his fault that I had fallen under the influence of some misogynistic shoe designer.

The shoes came off as soon as we reached the lobby of our building, and I happily walked the corridor with my feet, albeit bare, securely back on the ground. I was still alive. I felt like the winner on *Survivor*.

Note to self: next time you receive an invitation to a charity ball, send a donation. It's cheaper and much, much safer.

High Maintenance

This will be short and sweet because I have to run off to a doctor's appointment. I don't remember if it's the dermatologist or the ophthalmologist. I'll have to consult my calendar, so I don't wind up waiting an hour in the wrong office.

I also must check my wallet to make sure I replaced my insurance card after the last doctor's visit, and that I have cash, check, or credit card for the co-pay. Oh, and I'd better verify the status of my underwear, just in case today's appointment turns out to be with the gynecologist.

I used to look forward to the end of summer. I happily anticipated the cooler weather and the fact that my children were returning to school. Now summer's end has a whole new meaning. It has turned into check-up season.

My car also receives regular check-ups. But I take it to one place, and they examine all the moving parts. People, on the other hand, are required to see specialists. Hence, I'm spending the equivalent of an entire month rotating among medical offices.

I don't think it's my imagination, but with every passing year the maintenance list seems to grow longer. This year I added a retinologist, who, after the exam, suggested I see my ophthalmologist who will, no doubt, send me to an optometrist. Last year I added a cardiologist. Or was that the year before?

Some visits I don't mind so much. For example, seeing the dermatologist is definitely less stressful than a visit to the gastroenterologist. And the only preparation required is that I remove my makeup rather than the contents of my intestines.

The radiologist's office was kind enough to send me a postcard to remind me it was time for my annual mammogram. I'm not sure whether I will fit this in before or immediately after I see the dentist.

I also have a podiatrist on the payroll, but he had his turn last month. The periodontist shall have to wait until October. I would schedule the orthopedist, but he happens to be on vacation.

Don't get me wrong. I'm not complaining, only observing. I'm grateful that, so far, all outcomes have been good. And I shall continue to do what it takes to keep it that way. I just don't understand how someone who feels so young could have body parts that are apparently so old.

I've made a list, and before September is over, I will have seen nine different doctors. Not bad for a person considered to be in very good health!

How Old Am I in Dog Years?

They say that, over time, people start to resemble their pets. Or is it the other way around, that over time pets start to resemble their people? ("They" say so many things, who can keep it straight?) I don't know if this adage is necessarily true in my case, but I wouldn't mind if it was. My two dogs are beautiful. On the other hand, I'm not sure how they would feel if they began to resemble me.

While our respective visages may not have merged over the fourteen years we've been together, we have noticeably begun to share other physical changes. For example, my dogs can no longer jump in and out of the back of our SUV and require a helping boost. While I, myself, have never actually been required to jump in and out of the back of an SUV, I have the equivalent difficulty simply launching myself out of bed each morning. What I'm apparently sharing with my beloved pets are all the signs of aging.

Then there is the matter of graying hair. I was able to live comfortably in a state of denial for a long time, thanks to chemistry. However, my male dog, Davis—whose coat is golden brown—has, for several years, been sporting a white snout and head, and speckles throughout the rest of his body. He is immediately identifiable as an older dog and gets such comments as, "He looks good for his age." Since I now no longer dye my own hair, I can only hope that that remark could apply equally to both of us.

My female dog, Bette, who is one year younger (or should I say one year "less old?") than the male, was white to begin with. Therefore, she hasn't suffered the indignity of nature's highlights. However, like me, she does suffer from arthritis. And, like me, this causes her to limp. Her limp is persistent, though, while mine is only occasional. Though she walks around looking like she would benefit from a cane, she remains in high spirits and does the best she can. I, on the other hand, tend to whine.

Bette is on medications to relieve her symptoms. One of those medications, which I originally thought was strictly canine, turns out to be the very same drug that a friend of mine takes for his aching back. When the vet told me that I should fill Bette's second prescription at the pharmacy, I was convinced that the art of veterinary healing had really crossed a line.

Off I went to CVS to get my dog some relief, with a prescription that merely indicated my last name.

"Is this for you?" the pharmacy assistant asked, staring at her computer.

"No," I answered, hoping this would go no further. But she continued.

"Patient's first name?" she queried.

"Bette."

"Date of birth?"

I provided my dog's birthday. At this juncture, the pharmacy assistant finally lifted her eyes from the keyboard. She appeared a little startled.

"But that would make her only thirteen years old. How sad that she needs these pills."

"She's a dog," I stated, in my most matter-of-fact manner.

"Oh." She took a moment to process this information and then replied, "You know, your insurance won't pay for this." I acknowledged this unfortunate fact as I took out my credit card.

Oh, and did I mention that Bette also takes a pill to prevent bladder leakage? I suppose an additional tablet is less humiliating than doggie Depends. As for me, I simply try not to sneeze too hard.

I believe my older dog, Davis, has developed a hearing loss. Several years ago, my husband also developed a hearing loss. Repetition of verbal communication has become the norm in my household, if I'm to expect any type of response. However, there is a major difference between Davis and my husband. The dog cannot keep saying, "What?"

Together, we are experiencing other age-related changes, as well. Climbing stairs has become more of a challenge for them and may become so for us. Our walks in the park have become shorter and slower due to their diminished endurance. But these strolls are still an anticipated daily pleasure. And, lately, I'm finding the shorter duration and more leisurely pace quite compatible with my own preferred tempo.

Their vision is probably not as acute as it once was, but they are not yet bumping into things. And happily, neither am I.

In the park, I watch younger dogs running and chasing balls, and say to my pets, "Remember when you used to do that?" I also watch younger people jogging with ease, and say to myself, "Remember when you used to do that?"

Occasionally, Bette will forget her stiffness as something compels her to break into a run. This lasts for about ten seconds before she slows down again, resumes her hobble, and wears an expression that says, "What was I thinking?" I know that feeling. It occurs every time I try to catch a bus.

When we first brought our puppies home, they were much younger than we were. But, as dogs will, they have caught up. They have become our contemporaries, and we, theirs.

There is a certain beauty to be found in sharing our "golden" years with them. In many ways, life has taken on a mellowing that wasn't there before. And, in the fourteen years we've been together, we have never felt closer.

Recently, Bette has begun laser treatments to relieve her arthritis. The vet suggested that I might try the same.

Going forward, I know that I will agree to any treatment within reason to assure that my dogs are comfortable and maintain any possible residual of their youthful aura. But, love them as I do, if there's an allocation in the budget for cosmetic surgery, that belongs to *me*.

Dinner with Friends

Do you remember when dining out with friends was nothing more than an enjoyable way to spend an evening? When choosing a restaurant depended only on the type of food you preferred to eat that night, and where your table was located may have been a preference, but not necessarily a deal-breaker? When noise level was not a major consideration, and every few sentences of conversation was not interrupted by someone on the other side of the table saying, "What?" When the waiter did not have to repeat the specials three times, and then move around the table, and recite them three times again? When your biggest problem was finding a babysitter?

Those were the good old days before dinner with friends became a negotiation.

The process still begins with a phone call to make the date. Your friend suggests trying the new Italian restaurant, Cosi Fan Tutti. "Hold on," you say. You check with your husband. He wants to know if it is going to be one of those loud places. You ask your friend. She doesn't know; she hasn't yet been there. You tell him she doesn't know. Next question: are the waiters real Italians? Your friend asks, "What difference does that make?" He says, "If it's noisy, and they have accents, forget about it!"

Okay. She relents, and suggests we go back to the place where we ate last time. What's it called…The Quilted Alligator? "Honey, how about the Quilted Alligator again? The waiters are mostly American, except the one from Kazakhstan, and we can try to avoid him." He says that's fine, but he'll only go there if we can get the round table on the right that's up two steps in the other room.

And you remind your friend that before she makes the reservation, she should ask if they changed the light bulb in the chandelier like they promised so you don't have to bring your flashlight to read the menu.

"What time would you like to go?" your friend asks, starting to sound a bit exhausted. You ask if six-thirty is okay.

"Make it seven," she says. She doesn't like to sit with the early birds. She checks with her husband. No later, he says, or else he gets heartburn.

They offer to drive and will pick you up at six-forty-five. Your friend says not to worry, that her husband has finally gotten some new eyeglasses that do wonders for his night vision. You recall the last time he drove after sundown, and you felt lucky to get home alive. You take some comfort in the fact that it's daylight savings time. And if it's really dark on the way home, the wife always drives.

You think that the plans are finally set when the phone rings again. It's your friend, asking if it's okay if the Browns join us for the evening. You call out to your husband to ask if he minds if the Browns meet us at the restaurant. He says that's fine but only if she sits on his right side. You want to know why this is important. He reminds you that that's his good ear, and she has a soft voice.

You explain this to your friend, who promptly tells you that she didn't mind choosing the restaurant, making the reservation, requesting the table, providing the transportation, even asking about the light bulb. But she simply refuses to take responsibility for the seating arrangements. You don't blame her and decide it's probably not a good idea to remind her that you get a stiff neck if seated too close to an air-conditioning vent.

When all is said and done, you wonder if making dinner plans is worth it. Restaurants today have changed; they just don't seem to meet the criteria for a comfortable night out anymore.

You want someplace quiet and well-lit, and the room temperature is just right. Someplace where English is not the wait staff's second language, and the daily specials are printed in big letters right on the menu. Someplace nearby that you can reach on foot, so you don't have to drive when it's dark.

Perhaps it's best to stay at home and order in—at least until they start serving dinner at the Senior Center.

Withering Heights

Once upon a time there was a girl, who, at the age of thirteen, had reached her adult height of five feet, six-and-a-half inches. She imagined that she towered over her friends, who at that point in time, had reached only five feet, two or five feet, three. As a result, she felt BIG. Perhaps not as big as Gulliver surrounded by Lilliputians, but at least as big as a horse in a herd of ponies, or a bass fiddle among cellos.

BIG was not a good thing to be at that age. Standing last in line with the one or two other "tall" girls was one thing but being behind the boys made her feel as awkward as Wilt Chamberlin at a Little People's convention. When they palled around with the boys, her friends looked cute. She did not look cute. She was too tall to be cute. But cute was what she wanted to be. She hated her height.

Fortunately, as the girl emerged from the self-loathing early teen years, she learned to embrace her vertical dimension. She gave up her round-shouldered posture in favor of erectness. Her height gave her confidence, a certain strength. Now she was glad not to be one of the petite girls. (Not that there is anything wrong with petite. Some of her best friends…) She no longer considered "cute" complimentary when applied to her. In fact, she wished she were taller, maybe five feet, eight or nine. She wore high heels, (In those days, she could wear high heels without a fear of falling over.) and no longer minded if she was taller than a male companion.

She worshipped statuesque women. She idolized Judith Jameson and longed to become her, or some other majestically tall and graceful African woman with close-cropped hair. But genetically, all she could manage was the close-cropped hair.

The girl, now a woman, eventually crossed that point of no return called middle-age. To ensure an ongoing state of wellness, physical check-ups were now a required annual event. She had learned to fast for two days before the appointment to lessen the devastation of confronting the number on the scale, which had this nasty habit of increasing each year. And the nurse had an equally nasty habit of weighing her before she took her clothes off. (She made a mental note not to get her exams in the winter.) Height measurement? Never gave it a second thought. That is, until the year that same nurse told her she was five feet, five. "No, I'm not," she responded with an air of indignation, "I'm *at least* five-six."

"Sorry, dear," the nurse said, "like the scale, the ruler doesn't lie."

Fast forward to the present. Obviously, the girl in the fairy tale is yours truly. Now well past middle age (unless my life span increases to one hundred and forty years), I have become victim to that malevolent force that each year causes weight to go up and height to go down. But where are the inches going? I haven't had to shorten my pants or my skirts, so I'm fairly confident that my legs aren't shrinking. Therefore, it must be that my torso is disappearing—you know, that space between the breasts and the hips. If this trend continues, will my boobs one day be resting on my waist? Now there's a challenge for Victoria's Secret—speaking of which, I hate those models!

Like Jonah or Job, I wonder if I have been inflicted with a biblical punishment for being a whiny teen or an adult with too much tall pride? Or is it simply time compressing my spine? Does it matter? I am doomed to spending my last years looking up at my granddaughters.

Having my height measured each year has given a new meaning to the term "acrophobia." Is there no way to reverse this trend? I'm thinking maybe Martha Stewart has the recipe for Alice's magical "Eat Me" cake. I will inquire. (Is it my imagination, or is Martha also looking shorter these days?)

I know that the secret to successful aging is accommodation, so I will adapt. I will learn to be happy with my new lesser stature. I will avoid standing near tall women. But I warn you, when I am ninety, if I hear one person say, "Look at that little old lady. Isn't she cute?" I swear I will lift my walker and with it, beat them over the head. Or whatever body part I can reach.

It's Just a Matter of Time

The other day I met a friend that I hadn't seen for a long time. "So," she asked, "are you still working?"

"No," I answered, "I've recently retired."

"So," she asked again, "how have you been spending your time since you retired?" She might as well have asked me to explain Einstein's Theory of Relativity because, as I opened my mouth to respond, I found that, in fact, I could not. Respond, that is. The truth was, that although the days seemed to be passing quickly, I couldn't account for my time.

This was startling. When I worked and had family responsibilities, I could tell you (although I have no idea why you would be interested) that I would be grocery shopping on Wednesday evenings at six and folding laundry two nights a week at eleven. (In fact, one of the things I promised myself in retirement was to never again be folding laundry at eleven o'clock at night!)

So, what was I doing with all this precious time I had been given? It would seem that in my present life, organization had been replaced by chaos. So, I decide to follow myself around for a day and record my activities. I would not be caught again with my mouth agape, unable to respond to a simple query. The next time someone asked me what I did all day, I would be ready!

- 6:30 – I think I am awake.
- 7:15 – I am now fairly sure that I'm awake and decide to test this hypothesis by actually getting out of bed. Go to kitchen to start coffee and feed dogs. Dogs are grateful.
- 7:30 to 8:00 – Spend half-hour cleaning coffee grounds out of silverware drawer, into which I accidentally dump the coffee grinder. Not quite as awake as I thought.
- 8:00 to 8:30 – Prepare and eat breakfast for husband and self without further incident. I believe husband is grateful. Can't really tell. His face is buried in newspaper.
- 8:30 to 9:00 – Clean up breakfast dishes, shower, and dress. No appointments today, so can't think of a good reason to apply make-up.
- 9:00 to 10:00 – Load dogs into car and go to park for a walk. Very pleasant part of the morning. Dogs think so, too.
- 10:15 – Got laundry started.
- 10:30 – Go to desk and turn on computer. Open bookkeeping program to pay bills. Program not responding. Call the help line number.
- 11:00 – Am still listening to Montovani playing the best of the Beatles while holding for a representative. A man's voice is thanking me for holding and assuring me that my call is very important to them and will be answered in the order in which it was received.

(Sometimes when you call a large company, a woman's voice assures you that your call is very important to them. I wonder whose voice is more reassuring—a man's or a woman's? Spend about forty-five seconds wondering.)

- 11:30 – Finally connect to India. No wonder it took so long. My man in Mumbai talks me through steps to fix the problem. Adjust to his accent and ask him to repeat himself only three or four times. Problem could not be fixed. Purchase updated version of program. Spend additional time getting my credit card information and installing new program all the way from Mumbai. Amazing. Spend further additional time downloading old information onto new program. Have become very good friends with man from Mumbai. Regret not having applied make-up.

- 1:00 – Am off the phone. Spend next hour finally getting bills paid.

- 2:00 – Feeling hungry and realize I didn't eat lunch. Also realize I forgot to put laundry into dryer. Do so and begin a new load. Go out to get something to eat.

- 3:00 – Go back to computer and respond to emails.

- 4:00 – Take dogs out for afternoon walk. Start to think about dinner. Stop at supermarket.

- 5:00 – Put second load into dryer. Feed dogs. Begin to prepare dinner.

- 6:30 – Have dinner, clean up. Decide to go to a movie.

- 10:00 – Home. Let dogs out before bed. Watch a little TV.

- 10:45 – About to fall asleep. Leap out of bed. Forgot something.

- 11:00 – Folding laundry.

If I Should Die Before You . . .

Please don't stop reading. I promise that, despite the title, what follows is not a downer. Rather, it's an observation, a practical consideration, and maybe even a little bit funny.

What precipitated my seemingly ghoulish reflection was an actual conversation I had with my husband, a semi-retired attorney, who, for the past three years has been vowing that this year would be the last. However, you did notice that the prefix is still attached to the adjective.

But before I relate the conversation, let me set the scene. One recent morning, I took a risk and stepped into his home office. Why a risk, you might ask. Because upon crossing the threshold there is imminent danger of tripping over stacks of file folders, slipping on fallen pens, and getting vertigo as you observe the chaos surrounding his person as he sits on the small loveseat, diligently engrossed. He is unaware that our little dog, Sam, has been busy removing crumpled papers from his overflowing waste basket and turning them into confetti.

I, of course, notice this immediately, as I silently strategize about the best way to maneuver the vacuum cleaner so as not to disturb the piles. Forgetting why I put my life on the line in the first place, my focus is now on the waste basket. And so, the dialogue begins:

"Ahem, honey…" I say and he looks up. "I can't help but notice that the waste basket is brimming over, and the dog is engaged in an arts and crafts project."

"Oh, right," he says. "If you would get me a garbage bag, I'll empty it right now."

Get him a garbage bag? My feminist dander is rising. I know he's busy, but he will eventually take a break, and then he can get his own #S@&%* garbage bag!

Fortunately, however, before I go on a rant about liberation, it occurs to me that in fact, he may have no clue as to where to locate said item. And so instead I kindly say, without a hint of sarcasm, "Sweetheart, if I should die before you, let me show you where the garbage bags are kept."

I like to think we have a modern marriage, one in which responsibilities are shared. And in many ways, we do. For example, in matters financial, where my ability with numbers is limited to simple addition—with a calculator—I'm most appreciative that my darling can guide us through the big decisions.

But in matters of the household, despite my emancipation, I'm afraid we revert to more traditional roles. And when the time arrives that I must relinquish my role as domestic goddess, I do want him to be prepared. So, to ensure a somewhat easier transition, for I know that he will miss me terribly, I'm compiling a list of need-to-know items. As I am still very much here, l refer to it as my version of a living will.

If I should die before you, let me show you…
- how to load the dishwasher
- how to sew a button on your shirt
- how to put the draw string back in your sweatpants after you pull too hard and yank it out
- where we keep the light bulbs
- how to change a light bulb
- where we keep the dog food
- where to put the recyclables
- how to replace the ink in your printer
- where to look when you can't find your glasses
- where to look when you can't find the TV remote
- where to find a new tube of toothpaste or a fresh bar of soap
- how to order stuff on Amazon
- how to reboot the computer
- how to clean the lint trap in the dryer
- that there is a lint trap in the dryer
- that there is a dryer, and a washer
- where we keep the toilet paper…

This list is by no means exhaustive. It is a work in progress, to be added to as other gaps in knowledge become apparent. I know this is not a happy topic, but there is a great deal of comfort in knowing that after I'm gone, my darling will be able to replace that used cardboard cylinder with a brand-new roll.

Perhaps this essay will inspire other couples to compile a list of their own. I certainly hope so. In the meantime, while I am still alive, let me not forget to show him where the garbage bags are.

The Right to Bare Arms

Overheard at Saks:
    Shopper No. 1: "Ooh, that's such an adorable dress."
    Shopper No. 2: "So why don't you try it on?"
    Shopper No. 1: "Are you crazy? It's sleeveless!"

As we approach the warmer weather, I am convinced that this scene will be replayed over and over again in boutiques and department stores across the country. I don't know if this fixation transcends continents, but American women of a certain age have a thing about their arms.

Typically, it is not the entire arm. The arm between the elbow and the wrist may be entirely acceptable. It is the area that lies between the shoulder and the elbow, otherwise known as the upper arm, that is the offending body part.

This female upper-arm obsession was brought into sharp focus the other night when I was having dinner with some women friends, all contemporaries. Somehow the conversation became rerouted from the threat of global warming to apparel without sleeves. At the time, I wondered how we got from one topic to the other. But in retrospect, I can see a certain logic to this detour.

One after the other, my friends related how they long ago decided it was not in their best interest to display their upper arms. When even the most petite among us claimed that she was starting to feel bad about her elbows, I knew that this fixation had gone way too far! *OMG*, I thought. *Upper arms have become the new neck!*

As the only person at the table who still dared to go bare, I could sense seeds of doubt scattering through my psyche. Was I seeing my own arms through rose-colored glasses? Or maybe one of those fun-house mirrors that make you look long and thin? (Every woman should have one in her home.)

Although I have been a dedicated triceps toner, perhaps the jiggly, Jell-O look had finally caught up with me. I immediately reached for my sweater and blamed my cover-up on the excessive use of air-conditioning, so common in south Florida establishments. And yes, wasn't it awful how they kept these places so cold? Needing an objective opinion about the true state of my upper arms, I naturally turned to my husband.

"Honey," I said (I admit, I only call him Honey when I want support rather than the truth), "what do you think about my arms?"

"Your arms? I haven't given much thought to your arms."

"My upper arms. Do you think they're in good shape?"

"As compared with who?"

After correcting his grammar, I recounted the conversation at the dinner table. He made an enormous effort not to laugh, patted my shoulder, and told me I had nothing to worry about. Once again, the term of endearment had yielded the desired result. But I quickly turned to make sure the shoulder pat had not triggered any excess fatty tissue disturbance.

So, as older women we hate our upper arms. But it doesn't stop there. I bet we're not too crazy about our knees, either. Summer's coming. That's when we all get seasonal affective disorder. Every time we put on a bathing suit, we each have an opportunity to hate our entire body.

I don't know about men, but women tend to be very hard on themselves. We carry around criteria for perfection based on some long-ago, presently unachievable body image. Hey, why can't I just say, "My arms look great for my age," and be satisfied with that?

But there are some braver souls among us.

I was in a clothing store the other day, and because of my recent obsession with upper arms, noticed this very attractive "older" woman. She was of medium height, not particularly thin, with beautifully styled gray hair. Her make-up was well applied, she wore interesting earrings, and yes, she was sleeveless!

Believe me, she would not be hired for a deodorant ad, or any other product requiring one to bare their arms, yet there I was, admiring her appearance.

Good for you, lady, I thought. *It's a hot day. Why not?*

And so, Michelle Obama, don't get me wrong. I truly admire you. But you have set a standard for upper-arm fitness that few of us can match.

Therefore, if Hillary had made it to the White House, I was sure looking forward to her rolling up her sleeves!

Before and After

The other night, in a restaurant, my husband happened to encounter a woman he knew from high school days. This is not unusual. My husband frequently runs into people from his youth. In fact, I once wrote about this phenomenon, which never fails to amaze me. Growing up in a small town, his high school class had about 150 students, while mine, big city girl that I was, had about 1,000. Yet, I run into no one. But I digress. He introduced me to his former classmate, a very attractive woman who had to be my husband's age. Even if she was one of the smart kids and had skipped a few grades, she could only be a couple of years younger. So, we chatted politely (they chatted; I just smiled pleasantly and tried to look interested) then went our separate ways.

When we were seated at our table, my husband turned to me and said, "She used to be very pretty." What? Were we looking at the same woman? Had something gone awry with his new lens implants? The attractive woman I just met *was* very pretty. Right here, right now, in this very restaurant.

Of course, my husband was remembering a sixteen-year-old version of Dolores, whose name I changed to protect the VIC (Victim of Insulting Comment). The Dolores he recalled did not have laugh lines around her eyes, creases around the mouth, nor age spots on the hand he shook.

Come on. People get older. It's what they do. So why judge a woman's appearance by some outdated standard that clearly no longer applies? No seventy-something-year-old female is going to look like a fresh-faced cheerleader. Nor should they be expected to. And speaking for myself, I don't want to.

How often have I heard this "used to be" phrase applied, usually by a man, to an older actress who, in her younger days, was considered "hot." But if she has dared not to have boob lifts, Botox, or skin resurfacing (ouch!) she is cast aside. Why are they still idolizing the pin-up version, but failing to apply a different aesthetic today?

I know I'm joining the voices of all those who decry our youth-worshipping culture, but I find that frame of reference really irritating, both intellectually and emotionally. And I swear that my ire has absolutely nothing to do with the fact that I just had another birthday. And speaking of birthdays, on which birthday does a woman stop looking pretty, or hot, or beautiful, and start looking "good for her age?"

Looking good for one's age. There's another expression that deserves some scrutiny. What exactly does it mean to "look good for one's age?" Against what standard is the recipient of this compliment being judged? And, by the way, to say one looks good for one's age is hardly a compliment. Telling someone they look good should not require a qualifier.

If I am seventy-five and look good for my age, does that mean other seventy-five-year-olds do not look good? Does that mean that my cohorts are largely unattractive? And today, what does seventy-five look like anyway? Certainly not like my daughter, but I believe somewhat better than my grandmother.

"Age-defying" and "anti-aging,"—two more phrases that deserve the "delete" key. If you take a moment to examine them, what are they really saying?

Short of dying, it's not possible for a human being to defy age. Nor should we be asked to. And to be "anti-aging" is just not realistic, nor politically correct. Some of the best people I know are aging.

There is beauty at twenty and there is beauty at seventy, and we cannot expect them to be the same. As we age, gray hair, a few wrinkles, and some extra pounds should not be regarded as a disqualifier for seeing someone as very attractive.

In fact, when I look at photos of myself in high school, while I do see smoother skin and darker hair, I also see an insecure young woman who was struggling to find an identity. The person looking back at me in more recent photos is definitely older, but she is also someone with confidence, style, and a strong sense of who she is.

Society is harder on women than on men when it comes to aging. And we have more to overcome to feel good about ourselves. Yes, it's true. Life changes our appearance. But "pretty" should not have an expiration date.

(Okay, Sam the Dog, I feel better now. Let's go for a walk.)

April Is the Cruelest Month

April is a month that seems to inspire poetry. However, Chaucer, who praised April in his prologue to The Canterbury Tales would certainly not have agreed with the opening line of T.S. Eliot's famous poem, "The Wasteland," quoted in this essay's title. But then again, Chaucer was not a woman who had to face the terror and humiliation of shopping for a new bathing suit.

Neither I recognize, was T. S. Eliot, who nevertheless, with these five words, revealed a remarkable empathy with older women confronting the reality of the coming beach season. It is highly doubtful that this application of Eliot's words will be found in any serious literary criticism. This interpretation of their meaning is all mine.

For me, April is highlighted by a series of family visits, ending with the delightful company of our three youngest grandchildren, who are not so young anymore, and their parents. Spending a week with children in the warm April weather of South Florida means spending a lot of time in the water. Which means spending a lot of time in a bathing suit.

Up to this point, I had managed very nicely to avoid the heartbreak of too many revealed body parts. The weather had been cooperatively cool and not necessarily conducive to swimming. However, in the spirit of participating in their favorite activity, swimwear was definitely the dress code.

Oh, I do have a favorite bathing suit that I tolerate rather well. I bought it several years ago. It is one of those one-piece "miracle suits," designed to make you look ten pounds thinner. Or not. However, it manages to embrace my boobs in a manner which does not make me look like I require milking and covers enough pelvis to avoid the need for a Brazilian wax treatment.

While not particularly sexy, neither is it dowdy. Somewhere between Victoria's Secret and Talbot's, leaning heavily towards Talbot's.

But much to my horror, one day during my week as Esther Williams (millennials—you can Google her or whatever you do to resurrect dead film stars), my no-fault, default swimsuit developed a big, fat hole!

The meaning of this discovery did not escape me. I was going to need a new bathing suit. I think one must be a female of at least middle age to fully comprehend the trauma inherent in this situation.

I postponed this most-tortuous-of-all shopping experiences while I practiced holding in my stomach on a single breath for as long as possible. When I was satisfied that I could get an adequate result without passing out, I knew it was time. But first, I needed to tend to my hair and makeup. If I'm going to be made to feel my worst, at least let me look my best.

How does one choose a bathing suit store? We of a certain age are advised to look for a shop that has a good fitter. "What is a good fitter?" you might well ask. In the vernacular of the bathing suit world, this is a woman who is experienced in minimizing fleshy breasts and muffin tops, and the myriad of other possible bodily flaws. She will navigate you past the rows of tankinis (too much midriff reveal), bikinis (too much everything reveal), and straight down the aisle to the one-piece suits with magical concealing properties, and the ability to lift and tuck. After all, she knows that you've had it with sassy and sexy. You just need one that fits!

As I perused the racks where no teenager would be caught dead, I listened to her helpful suggestions about necklines, pleats, solids, or prints. I stared at my choices in dismay. I rejected the flowery print which reminded me of a cloth for a picnic table I once purchased at Bed, Bath and Beyond, and also decided to forgo the animal print, which I feared would make me look like a pregnant cheetah. Thus, as in life, in the world of one-piece bathing suits, you can't go wrong with basic black.

I bravely entered the fitting room, armed with several variations of black swimsuits in a size recommended by the fitter, which happens to be a size larger than any other clothing that I own.

Great. Just keep heaping on the humiliation.

I stripped to my undies and began the try-on process. Yuck! What was I thinking? Next! Finally, there was the magic suit. It was cut just right, reduced the tummy, and camouflaged a variety of imperfections. But, I noticed, it was a little too big. Summoning the fitter, I triumphantly requested the suit in a smaller size. I waited ten minutes while she searched and returned with the bad news that they didn't have another one. Sorry.

Well, that's that, I thought. *I did my best. I'll just have to go home and continue to practice inhaling my stomach. Besides, my grandkids have all left. I can postpone the unpleasant outing for another day.*

There was, I discovered that same night, a bright side to this experience. While I was switching channels among the various news stations, I had the opportunity, or misfortune, of seeing representatives from both political parties ranting at each other. What I would normally have found excruciatingly annoying, now produced a broad grin. Obsessed as I was with the events of the day, I imagined each of them, including the moderator, standing front and center, and each was dressed in a bathing suit. How's that for an equalizer? Why, it's almost poetic.

Now You See Me, Now You Don't

I was in a doctor's waiting room the other day, catching up on my magazine reading, when the title of a particular article captured my attention: "The Disappearance of Older Women."

Had this been the *National Enquirer*, I would likely have assumed that it was another story about alien abductions. But why aliens would want to kidnap post-menopausal females was indeed a mystery unto itself. Perhaps on some planet not yet discovered by NASA they had overbuilt their assisted living facilities? Even for the *Enquirer*, that seemed a little far-fetched.

As I continued waiting in the space designated for this purpose, I had ample opportunity to delve further into this article to discover that in fact, it was a lament. Written by an attractive middle-aged woman (judging from her photo which may or may not have been retouched), she was somewhat bitterly expounding the fact that women, once they reach the age of fifty, become invisible.

Blaming this phenomenon on a youth-obsessed society, she went on to cite examples from her recent experiences which made her feel that she was no longer vital or important or noticeable by others.

She stated that men didn't look up when she walked into a room. She went largely unnoticed by passersby on the street. She could no longer hold the glance of a thirty-year-old man on the subway. Gone were her attractiveness and sex appeal, all washed away with the last flow of menstrual blood (my words, not hers). She believed herself to be in a slow, lingering decline.

Wow! Give that woman some Prozac and save some for me. This was indeed very serious. Had I, too, become invisible but was too busy being busy to notice?

I tried to recall the last time I had walked past a construction site to the sound of cat calls emanating from under the hard hats. Many years ago, probably, and even then, I recall he was a good deal older and most likely had cataracts.

As I checked more deeply into this phenomenon, I discovered not just other articles on the same topic, but also actual studies proving that women of a certain age shared this sense of becoming invisible. And it seems that the primary cause is no longer being acknowledged by men. If this is true, how sad that our self-esteem is so dependent upon male attention. But nevertheless, I think I might have discovered at least a temporary antidote.

Older women, want to *not* be invisible? Want to be noticed by men, particularly younger men? Then wander through the cosmetics section of a department store or stroll past a boutique selling expensive anti-aging products, and I promise you, you will get more attention than Megyn Kelly at a Donald Trump rally.

This is what happened to me. We were enjoying a visit from our beautiful twenty-four-year-old granddaughter and her twenty-four-year-old boyfriend. (Should I feel badly that he didn't try to flirt with me, or ask me to run away with him?) I had taken them for a stroll on a famous shopping street in our town, noted for its beautiful architecture and unaffordable clothing.

Standing outside of one of the boutiques was a man, probably in his thirties, dressed in a suit, shirt, and tie, all of which was black. His hair was black, his skin was swarthy, and his face sported a five o'clock shadow, not the grungy, but the sexy kind. As we passed by, he spoke. An exotic foreign accent added to his sex appeal. I noticed all of this but paid it little mind until I realized he was speaking not to my beautiful granddaughter, but to me!

He laughed, he joked, he teased; he was utterly charming. He was totally into me. I was the opposite of invisible! I was a target.

Next thing I knew, I was practically yanked into the store and seated in a chair. He whipped out an elegantly packaged tube of cream which he proceeded to apply under my left eye. He extolled its magical powers, how it would instantly reduce the wrinkles and puffiness, giving me a much younger appearance. When he was done, he held up a mirror so that I might witness this miracle for myself.

I compared my two eyes, and told him I preferred my right eye, as the skin under my left eye still looked the same but was now greasy. He did not appreciate my humor, nor my lack of interest in his product. I was summarily dismissed.

He stepped back outside to stalk his next invisible woman.

Afterwards, I had to laugh at myself for enjoying this little bit of flirtatious exchange with a handsome "younger" man, even if he was trying to empty my wallet by selling me some ridiculously expensive products that falsely promise to make me look like my granddaughter's big sister.

So, would I trade the confidence and self-awareness that aging has provided for a few more whistles from a construction worker? Absolutely not. There's freedom in no longer requiring that kind of approval. And there is freedom in being invisible. Perhaps attention is highly overrated.

Failure to Print

Honestly, did I really need another reminder that I was old?

I thought I paid my dues this year with a few more wrinkles, deeper frown lines, a couple of extra sunspots, and a pair of eyeglasses that I was now required to use when driving. Oh, and the addition to my never-again list of a few more foods that give me indigestion.

So, did I have to suffer yet another indignity of aging, in front of a complete stranger, no less?

No, I didn't lose bladder control. I lost my fingerprints! Let me explain how this came to light.

My husband and I had applied for the Global Entry Pass that is supposed to make air travel a little easier. If you have this card, you can bypass the lines at security and immigration by checking yourself in or out using a special kiosk. Whether this method is preferable to being escorted in a wheelchair remains to be seen.

In any event, since neither of us could justify needing a wheelchair just yet, we thought we would obtain these cards, and become official "trusted travelers."

Part of the process of qualifying for this privilege is an in-person appointment at an office of U.S. Customs and Border Protection. We were interviewed by a friendly, uniformed officer. (I think they're called "officers." Or maybe they're called "agents?" I'm not sure. In any event, he was friendly.) We responded to the routine questions and each of us in turn had our pictures taken. So far, so good.

Also required was a set of fingerprints. They don't use ink pads anymore. Instead, fingerprints are recorded biometrically using computers and a scanner. It's simple, really. All you have to do is place four fingers on a piece of glass and the computer reads your prints. Reads *your* prints, maybe, but unfortunately, not mine. The nice gentleman tried again, then again. But neither my left nor right hand would yield a set of readable, unsmeared fingerprints.

I became concerned. Had I contracted some exotic disease that was slowly stripping away my identity? But this formerly nice man tells me not to worry. This frequently happens with old people. Old people!!!

Apparently, he explains, as we age, our skin loses elasticity. (Every woman knows that already!) The ridges that form our prints get thicker, and the height between the top of the ridge and the bottom of the furrow gets narrow, so there is less prominence.

The problem was eventually solved by applying lotion to my fingertips, which magically allowed the scanner to take its impression. I'm informed that I might have to apply lotion each time I use a Global Entry kiosk. Otherwise, it may not work. Great! My Global Entry Pass that was supposed to eliminate some of the stress of traveling has just added a new anxiety. Maybe I'll opt for the wheelchair after all.

But having this knowledge isn't very helpful. I'm still left with the sorry news that I'm an old person with one less distinctive feature and left wondering what comes next. And it's not particularly comforting to know there are others like me. Someone or something has played an ironic prank. Or else, why would time remove the creases from where we need them, and add new creases where we don't? It saddens me that Mother Nature isn't perfect. Either that, or she possesses a very wicked sense of humor.

Generation _____?

It occurred to me the other day that I was invisible. Not just me, but my entire generation. It appears that we lack importance. I'm basing this rather sad conclusion on the fact that we have been entirely overlooked by the folks who bestow catchy cohort labels.

Let's get specific. At the risk of revealing my true age, which most of you already know, I'm referring to those of us born between 1927 and 1945. Admittedly, I have steel wool in my brain when it comes to math, but according to my calculations, we number almost twenty-eight million (2010 U.S. census), and yet we go about our daily lives without a cultural tag. And personally, I'm feeling a bit resentful. What kind of legacy is this to leave to our children and grandchildren, otherwise known as the Xs and the Ys, and possibly the Zs?

Born too late to be World War II heroes, and too early to be a part of the post-war birth explosion, we have wound up sandwiched awkwardly between the Greatest Generation and the Baby Boomers. An entire generation without a context!

No doubt a result of having too much time on my hands, I decided to delve into this matter a bit further. Perhaps understanding the genesis of other generational labels would allow me to suggest something clever and catchy for my own. Something that would acknowledge the faceless twenty-eight million. Something that might fit neatly as a crossword puzzle response or a question on *Jeopardy*!

Well, thanks to Tom Brokaw, who himself, happens to be one of the faceless, those born between 1901 and 1926 were widely lauded as the Greatest Generation. I don't disagree. They survived the Depression and fought the second world war. They deserve the recognition, but come on, Tom, whatever happened to taking care of your own?

And the hype about the Baby Boomers? Aren't you just sick of it? Those born between 1946 and 1964 think they're so special. And who can blame them with all the attention they've always gotten from the media and the marketers. Big deal. You've earned a lot of money and went to Woodstock. But you have no exclusive claim to rock 'n roll, civil rights, or feminism. Some of us latter-born question marks were right there with you.

Generation-naming just kept moving forward, leaving us further in the dust. Soon there was Gen X, a term with literary roots co-opted once again by Madison Avenue. Covering roughly the years 1966 to the early 80s, the X originally meant that the fate of this generation was unknown. Gen Y was so-called because it was the next letter of the alphabet. These folks are also known as the Millennials because the majority come of age after the turn of the century. There are actually more of them than there are Boomers.

But I'm getting a little sick of the attention they're getting, as well, with all the tweeting and Instagramming, and the me-me-me attitude. But what else can you expect from a generation that won ribbons just for showing up? All of that self-centeredness, however, does not make them ineligible for a unique identity, even if the word "millennial" does evoke visions of a multi-legged insect.

And have you heard about Gen Z, also known as iGen? Born after 2001, and most barely old enough for a bar mitzvah, they already have the attention of the cultural pulse-takers, while their grandparents and great-grandparents slip further into obscurity.

All of which brings us to today when I'm sure somewhere someone is working hard at predicting the zeitgeist of a generation yet to be born and trying to figure out a catchy name.

So back to the predicament of the invisible twenty-eight million: surely there were significant events during our decades that would lend themselves to an overriding identity. For example, I've heard us referred to as the "Depression Babies" or the "War Babies," but those are such downers. Certainly, we can do better.

We are the generation that saw the end of Prohibition, the New Deal, Social Security, Superman, and sliced white bread. The truth be told, I discovered that my generation did, in fact, have a name. If you are not a sociologist, I challenge you to tell me what it is. I don't recall ever seeing it used in any type of popular media in my lifetime. If you were born between 1926 and 1945, welcome to the "Silent Generation."

The Silent Generation. How does that sit with you? Called thus because we didn't make waves, worked hard, and stuck by good old-fashioned values. All positive traits, I suppose, but so boring!

So as the Silent Generation, it seems fitting that we have gone unnoticed. And now that the truth has been revealed, however disappointing, perhaps it's time to move on to more important causes, such as discovering the true nature of Atticus Finch.

After all, "What's in a name?" asked Juliet, from her balcony in Verona. But at our age, should we really be debating existential questions with an iGen?

And Don't Call Me Elderly!

Thirty-seven years ago, before anyone would dare refer to me as elderly, a movie was released called *Airplane!* Starring Leslie Nielsen, this spoof of Hollywood disaster films became an unlikely sensation. Of the many brilliant sight gags and clever lines, the brief dialogue between Leslie Nielsen and Robert Hays, containing the "surely-Shirley" confusion, continues to bring a smile to my face.

Fortunately, over the intervening years, I've encountered very few women named Shirley, which has limited embarrassing moments for me (caused by uncontrollable giggling). And, finally, I can borrow the line, or at least, paraphrase it, to air a grievance.

I'd like to deliver a message to the media, and I am serious. *Don't call me elderly!* In fact, don't call me anything at all. If you must state my age in your story, it should not require a modifier.

Whenever a news story appears about a seventy-three-year-old, for example, he or she is invariably referred to as "elderly." In fact, they are often labeled as "elderly" before you are even told their age.

Here's an example. The headline states, "Elderly Woman Robs Bank." The story then goes on to report that Mamie Green, age sixty-nine, held up the Yucca City Bank at gun point, and eluded police by hiding in a tree. Now I ask you, should a sixty-nine-year-old woman who can wield a pistol, rob a bank, and climb a tree be called elderly?

Obviously, this example is fictitious and a bit silly, created to make a point. But there are very real examples. An NPR story reported on a seventy-one-year-old midwife and referred to her as "elderly." Elderly!? *Really?!!?* She's still working, delivering babies. There's nothing elderly about her, and these days, not even her age. And does labeling her as elderly enhance the story about midwifery? Totally irrelevant if you ask me. If the woman were fifty-five, would NPR have referred to her as "borderline middle-aged woman?"

If a woman of a certain age had the misfortune of getting hit by a bus, is that any more tragic than a forty-year-old being hit by a bus? Yet, you can be sure that the former would be cited as "Elderly Woman Gets Hit by a Bus," while the forty-year-old would merely be unlucky.

So, what does "elderly" mean, exactly? The dictionary defines "elderly" as *past middle age and approaching the rest of life; sometimes considered offensive.* The meaning of the word appears harmless enough. It's the connotation of the word that's damaging. In our culture, the word "elderly" carries the images of "frail," "feeble," and "dependent." And what robust seventy-five- or -six-year-old wants to be lumped into that stereotype?

I recognize that in some circles "elder" is not a four-letter word. If I were a member of a certain church, or a Native American tribe, being called an elder might be an honor. I would be a respected advisor, a bestower of wisdom, perhaps even a goddess.

But unfortunately, that's not the world in which most of us live. Instead, elderly is an ageist label.

You might think that none of this is important, but words do shape attitudes and responses. So, what word should we use instead? Geezer? Long in the tooth? Over the hill? Mature? Senior Citizen? Or simply, Old? I don't have the answer, and as far as I can tell, neither does anyone else.

I like to think that age is more a matter of how you feel rather than a number. Therefore, I ask not to be assigned to a category based on the year in which I was born.

So, Leslie Nielsen, rest assured. Although you were the advanced age of fifty-four when you made the career move from dramatic actor to comedy genius, I would never call you elderly.

Eye Opener

By any chance, do you to remember an old movie called *The Enchanted Cottage* starring Robert Young and Dorothy McGuire? It was released a long time ago, 1945 to be exact. If you don't remember it, please don't lie and tell me it's because you weren't born yet. I happen to know how old you are!

Anyway, in this film, Robert Young plays a disfigured war veteran and Dorothy McGuire plays a homely maid. The two marry, and as time passes, fall more deeply in love. Within the confines of the cottage in which they live, they begin to appear beautiful to each other.

Well, apparently, I had been happily living in an enchanted cottage of my own. At least until the other day, when a terrorist disguised as an eye doctor blew the whole thing to smithereens! You see (she punned), I recently had cataract surgery. No big deal, I hear you saying. Just another, inevitable part of the aging process. Everybody does it. So, if everybody does it, why didn't anyone *warn me?*

My eyes are considerably older than I am. And because of this, I accepted the fact that my reading glasses gradually got stronger, and I eventually needed distance glasses for driving. And at night I did notice that the headlights of oncoming cars had become more distracting. But I figured it was due to inferior workmanship.

So, you can imagine my surprise, when, at my last eye exam, the doctor suggested that I consider having my cataracts removed. What cataracts? *Who had cataracts?* Had he failed to mention this before, or was I just not listening?

Who knows for how many years these insidious little clouds had been gradually forming on the lenses of my eyes, and, unbeknownst to me, eventually caused me to view the world in a gauze-like haze? A little inconvenient at times, but actually, not unlovely. A little like a filter used on a camera to provide a mysterious, romantic ambiance. And because the change happens slowly, one does tend to adjust.

Nevertheless, I agreed to the surgery, one eye at a time. So, my left eye is now younger than my right, resulting in both good news and bad news. The good news is that I do see much better. The bad news is—that I see much better!

OMG! Would you just look at the kitchen floor! Where did all that dog hair come from? I mean, I was aware there was *some* dog hair from my two constantly shedding Labrador retrievers, but when did they start going bald? Since the surgery, I have progressed from running the vacuum every other day to every fifteen minutes.

When did the walls get so dirty? My new fashion accessory is a can of Ajax and a wet sponge. And look, the paint is chipping in the corner. And I wonder what caused the scratches on the bedroom floor? We really need to consider whether it's time for a new paint job, and having the floors redone. Or possibly moving.

But the excess of dog hair, dirty walls, chipped paint, and scratched floors were only foreplay for the granddaddy of all shockers.

The morning following the day of the surgery, my husband heard a blood-curdling shriek emanating from the bathroom. He sprang from the bed, probably believing that our bathtub had been occupied by an army of Palmetto bugs. Even one of those creatures would call forth a vocalization that could land me a role in a horror movie.

A tub-full of roaches having a spa day in my Jacuzzi would have been preferable. The true source of the shriek was the face in the mirror that was looking back at me. Apparently, during the night, I had channeled the late Dorian Gray.

Who was this stranger? She did look familiar, but the Susan I remembered did not have those pouches under her eyes, those deep laugh-lines around her mouth, the sagging jowls, and a neck that Nora Ephron would definitely feel bad about. And where did all those freckles come from? (Were they freckles or something worse?)

As terrifying as it was, I couldn't take my good eye off that face in the mirror. Whoever coined the phrase "reality bites" should receive a Pulitzer Prize. Truer words had never been spoken.

I've always been good in a crisis, so as calmness returned, I formulated a plan. There was help out there. I simply had to reach out to my friends whom, because they had been dealing with signs of aging much longer than I, knew the best repair people.

Later that day, the swelling under my eye did diminish significantly. Unfortunately, I can't say that for the rest of it.

In two weeks, I shall have the other eye done. I can only imagine what additional imperfections await me.

While it is miraculous, cataract surgery can be quite costly. Yes, insurance does cover the medical expenses. But even the best policies don't include house repainting, floor scraping, moving, or cosmetic procedures.

So, in the interest of parsimony, I'm considering an alternative to the costly cosmetic procedures. For the near future at least, I shall choose my companions more selectively. I will hang out only with those friends who still have cataracts. That way, they will still see me through the slightly foggy, but highly complementary filter, and together we can all return to The Enchanted Cottage.

Which, by now, could probably use a new paint job.

There's a Hole in My Bucket List

I don't have a bucket list. There, I said it.

I hope this confession will not strip away my senior citizen discounts. After all, it has taken me years to get here, and I deserve to ride for half-fare. But it had to be said. Even if I risk losing my benefits.

Having reached a certain age, I know I'm supposed to have one. In fact, just the other day a clever, but meddlesome, person suggested an item I might add to my bucket list, then looked at me with shock and disbelief when I told him that no such list existed. How could I possibly not have a catalog of unfulfilled wishes that must be achieved before I expire?

Oh sure, you can have a bucket list at any age. However, when the days ahead of you are fewer than the days behind, the wisdom is that one must hasten to fulfill every last dream. Who needs that pressure at this time of their life?

The truth is, I can't imagine lying on my deathbed, regretting that I had never gone zip lining. The truth is, I don't want to think about my deathbed at all. Or about zip lining. The image of me hanging from a thin wire makes my shoulders hurt.

The very notion of a bucket list is depressing. The term derives from the phrase "kick the bucket," which derives from the act of ending one's life by placing a noose around the neck, standing on a pail, tossing the rope around a rafter, and when the rope was securely fastened, kicking the bucket out from under. Definitely more fatal than zip lining.

Since that 2007 movie with Jack Nicholson and Morgan Freeman, the imperative to create a bucket list is so great that there are actually numerous websites to help the unimaginative among us compile a collection of foolhardy feats, places to visit, and dumb things to eat that may or may not actually bring your final day closer to reality.

Seeking inspiration, I perused some of these sites and found them very helpful. My bucket is no longer empty. It now contains at least 101 challenges I enthusiastically hope never to meet.

For example, I'm sure I can live happily for the rest of my life without the experience of sky diving. Much as I can live happily for the rest of my life without knowing what it feels like to get hit by a bus. I'm not afraid of heights but slipping off the couch onto a rug is about as much free fall as I care to experience. Ditto for hang-gliding, parasailing, and bungee jumping. I've already covered zip lining.

When I was younger, rock climbing and/or planting a flag on a high peak might have held some attraction. But at this point in life, the greatest physical challenge I care to accept is to once again be able to reach behind my back and fasten my bra.

I love sea life, but I'm not so crazy about water. So, scratch cliff-jumping, swimming with sharks, scuba diving, and surfing. I have been white water rafting and managed to come away unscathed, save for a mild case of PTSD, so I think I'd rather not push it.

Even though it's land-based, Zorbing holds minimal appeal. Rolling down a hill inside a large plastic ball serves little purpose except to experience the adrenaline rush of a hamster. I don't want to get a tattoo, although it might be interesting to adorn my body with more color variety than just brown spots. And nix the Brazilian wax. Call me modest, but I think I've passed the expiration date for undraping on a nude beach.

And if I died tomorrow, I'm positive I'd have no regrets about never sampling chocolate-covered grasshoppers, learning a new language, being chased by bulls, or taking tuba lessons. Life has been good so far, and I've had the privilege of doing many things and visiting many places. It's not that I've been everywhere and seen everything. It's just that whatever I have left undone is far from mandatory. And so, I remain list-less.

But how's this for an idea of what to do with that empty bucket? How about filling it with fried chicken, and inviting some like-minded friends for a finger-lickin' meal? And don't forget the pie and ice cream for dessert. If I could do this just once without food-guilt, I'm sure I would die a happy woman!

P.S. Come closer and I will admit to having a single item on my bucket list. That is, to be the oldest intern ever to join the writing team for *Saturday Night Live*. So, if you know someone who knows someone, would you be kind enough to put in a good word?

Summer Is a Bummer

Admittedly, I'm not a big fan of nostalgia. My capacity for fondly recounting the good old days is about half a cup. Sure, I have pleasant memories of growing up in the 40s and 50s, but I'm not about to initiate a petition for the return of Howdy Doody or lobby the fashion industry to bring back poodle skirts.

And, while I do miss Archie and Jughead, I don't get sentimental when reminded of what the price of gasoline used to be, or that a movie ticket used to cost 25¢.

While I pride myself for being a forward-thinking kind of gal, I must confess that this past Memorial Day weekend, the unofficial start of a new season, and the hot weather, combined to trigger images of childhood, and a good, old-fashioned, unfettered summer!

Whatever happened to the summers of my youth? I really do miss them. I miss the anticipation of them: the arrival of June, the end of school, the extended hours of daylight, and more time to spend outdoors.

While I still enjoy the extended hours of daylight, my appreciation is now more often from behind a screen door. Summers used to be carefree. Now they are hazardous to your health.

It's hard to enjoy summer when you are repeatedly reminded of all the risks that come with warm weather. How can I possibly find the same pleasures of the season when I feel I must carry my garbage to the outdoor bin wearing a hazmat suit? When did summer become dangerous?

Blame Covid, global warming, or the thinning of the ozone layer, but daring to walk out the front door unprotected feels like extreme risk-taking behavior. Perhaps that's why I experience an adrenaline rush if I go to my mailbox without a hat on. And the beach? A real downer. My inner child longs to run freely in and out of the water, and build elaborate sandcastles complete with moats. But my outer older person threatens me with more age spots and/or a trip to the dermatologist if I don't remain under the umbrella. Among my beach equipment is a tape measure to ensure that I am at least six feet away from the nearest beach blanket. And mask-wearing does result in a weird suntan.

Would I consider a drive in a convertible? Never. At least not until the sun goes down. And even with the top up, one is not safe. I've learned that bad rays can penetrate glass. Therefore, I'm seriously considering window treatments for my car.

And when it comes to applying sun protection, perhaps someone can help me with the proper protocol. Do I apply my sun block before or after I rub on my skin moisturizer? If I apply my moisturizer first, will that prevent my sun block from working? But if I apply my sun block first, will that prevent my moisturizer from plumping up my wrinkles?

In any event, there are now two layers of lotion on my face before I even put on my makeup. It's no wonder that I walk around for the rest of the day feeling like a stick of butter.

And remember when mosquito bites were simply that? Annoying little itchy bumps that would subside in a couple of days? Since malaria was not a serious threat for those of us growing up in Bensonhurst, mosquitoes, while never our friends, were not to be feared. And insects did not dictate how we dressed.

But in summer I am told that I must be cautious about the Zika virus. I have been warned to cover up and use insect repellent. Tell me, do I spray this on before or after the sunblock and skin moisturizer? One expert even suggested we wear mosquito netting to cover our faces. Hey, why not? It's the perfect fashion accessory for the surgical mask worn to protect us from air pollution and Covid.

And in the good old summertime, who ever heard of ticks? Ticks were a sound made by my grandfather's pocket watch. But I must also cover up and spray to prevent Lyme disease. So that's me, in ninety-degree weather, walking my dog in an outfit that looks like I'm about to embark on a ski vacation.

Maybe I should invest in that hazmat suit after all. I wonder, is it a one-size-fits-all, and does it come in a choice of colors?

I admit, summer still has some pleasures. I do look forward to fresh-picked corn, luscious tomatoes, and juicy summer fruit. However, please don't mind if I graciously decline that outdoor picnic for the safety and security of a screened in porch.

But as I watch my grandchildren from said screen porch, thoroughly enjoying their summer, and their mother chasing them with a tube of sunblock, another thought occurs to me. Summer hasn't changed at all. I have. Summer has always had its perils, but to be concerned about them was the responsibility of the adults.

I can recall my own mother's hesitance to venture out from under the umbrella when she reluctantly consented to go to the beach, something as I child I could never comprehend. Today, that shade-seeking grown-up is me.

My Left Shoulder

I apologize for the fact that I'm late in delivering this new essay. That is, if anyone even noticed that I'm a few days past my deadline. Five to be exact, if you happened to mark your calendar. Which I highly doubt. But that's okay. I don't mind my usual timeliness being taken for granted.

In case you're interested, I do have a good excuse. No, it's not "the dog ate my homework," or in this case, my essay. It's better than that.

One week ago, I had an encounter with an orthopedic surgeon. And while I was under, and totally helpless, he performed a total replacement of my left shoulder.

"OMG," I hear you gasp. But stay calm. It's not as dire as it sounds. Though not as common as rotator cuff repair, I believe a shoulder replacement is actually less stressful. Imagine a hip replacement closer to your neck. (Incidentally, if I might brag, my rotator cuff is in pristine condition, and apparently years younger than the rest of the left shoulder anatomy.)

The need for this particular fine-tuning of my bones and cartilage was not a sudden event. Rather, it was a gradual erosion (over several years) of my ability to use my left arm.

By the way, did I happen to mention that I am part of "the 10% of Americans?" Before you hit me up for a loan, let me be clear that I am not referring to my bank account, but to the fact that I'm left-handed. So, it figures that all the wear and tear would be on the left side, while the right hand has just been along for the ride.

And what was the source of this physical abuse? I'd like to say it was extreme tennis, or my early career as a discus thrower, but those would clearly be alternative facts. The simple, unglamorous truth is osteoarthritis. I have a left shoulder that has experienced many more birthdays than the rest of me!

Little things that I had always taken for granted were becoming stressful. For example, hooking my bra became a feat equal to competitive arm wrestling. And I was no longer able to sleep on my left side, which put me directly into the line of fire of the dissonant midnight serenade of my bed partner.

I had to quit golf this winter, which may actually qualify as a disguised blessing. My computer mouse has been resting on the other side of the keyboard for months now. And I became expert at the one-handed shampoo.

But I stoically persevered, trying to delay the inevitable. Although I must admit that it was growing tiresome, seeking out rest rooms where the toilet paper holder was located on the right. (And at times, even a little dangerous if the search took too long.)

However, we all have our tipping points. And mine came the morning I discovered the very inconvenient truth that I could no longer painlessly raise my left arm high enough to readily apply my eye makeup!

Call me vain, but could I really risk leaving the house with clumped eyelashes? Or eyeliner that no longer went on smoothly, but looked like a road in desperate need of repair? Time to go under the knife.

I understand that the surgery went very well, but what do I know? I was fast asleep. The big shocker upon awakening was that it felt like my entire left arm was missing. For an instant, I panicked. Had the surgeon done the repeal, but forgot to replace? Turns out I was merely feeling, or not feeling, the effects of a nerve blocker.

I won't bore you with the rest of the details. (Actually, I'd love to bore you, but it's too much trouble. I can only type with one finger.)

I'm home now, recuperating, and feeling pretty good. I'm stuck indoors for a while but keeping quite busy. Between icing my shoulder and doing my exercises, I hardly have time to go to the bathroom. Which still requires that the toilet paper be on the right side. At least for now.

And I'm now a card-carrying member of the spare parts club. I was actually given a small document to carry in my wallet. This is in case my new metal and plastic shoulder set off any airport security alarms. Hopefully, it will assure the TSA workers that I have no intention of imploding.

I have every expectation of a complete recovery and fully restored range of motion of my left arm. I look forward to resuming golf and perfectly applied eye makeup. And returning the computer mouse back to its rightful place on the left side of the keyboard as I once again type future essays on time with two hands.

The Insomnia Games

I am not, by nature, a competitive person. If I even so much as win at a game of Scrabble, my inclination is to leap over the board, hug the loser, and say, "sorry." Yet, each morning, upon opening my eyes, I find myself engaged in a verbal duel.

I'm not exactly sure when this all began. Perhaps it started on that critical birthday. The one when my bladder decided to stop cooperating with my need for hydration, and instead taunt me during the night in two-hour intervals. Which I think is very spiteful.

I'm reminded of my former dogs. When they were old, I had to remove their water bowls no later than five at night to prevent them from awakening after bedtime and having to go outside to pee. At least I don't have to go outside, but I'm definitely considering rolling back happy hour.

What is referred to as "a good night's sleep" has become elusive—as it has for my husband, who swears he hasn't slept through the night since he was ten months old. His parents are deceased so I cannot confirm or deny this report, but I do know that another factor in my *sleepus interruptus* is the glow of his iPad at some ungodly hour.

As a result of this pernicious insomnia, we have become quite competitive, constantly challenging each other as to who has had the worst night. A typical morning conversation might go something like this:

"How did you sleep?"

"Terrible."

"Yeah, well, I slept worse."

"I woke at three and haven't been to sleep since."

"Yeah, well, I woke at two-fifty."

"No, you didn't. I saw you. You were sound asleep."

"I was just pretending."

"So how come you were snoring?"

"I had to go to the bathroom three times."

"I had to go four."

"Yeah, well, I had leg cramps."

"I know. I heard you marching around the bedroom."

"No, you didn't. You were sleeping."

The verbal jousting is halted by the current dog, who is covering his ears, and our need for coffee. This requires one of us leaving the bed, usually me.

I'm quite sure that competitive not-sleeping isn't limited to us. I believe we have entered a stage in life when sleep deprivation may very well be the new status age-related deficit, edging out other contenders, like greatest number of body part replacements, who knows the best doctors, and HDL scores.

Conversations around a dinner table often focus on the virtues and pitfalls of Ambien over Lunesta, or how spraying lavender on your pillowcase is very soothing and will lull you to dreamland. I tried that. I wound up with a damp pillowcase and an allergy attack.

And don't ever complain to a friend that you're tired all the time because you average only four hours of sleep. Sympathy will not be forthcoming, but rather, "You think that's bad? I *never* sleep!"

As for me, I'm tired, and would like to withdraw from the game. I'd gladly relinquish the gold medal in exchange for a few nights of sound, solid, restful sleep. And when my husband laments in the morning about how bad the night was, I would gently pat his hand, commiserate, and try my best to refrain from gloating. After all, I'm not a competitive person.

Diary of a Dinner Date

*(Or: What Is Likely to Occur When Your Age
Exceeds the Speed Limit on Most US Highways)*

It began with a simple overture, an attempt to make a dinner date with friends. But there was no way I could foresee the chaos that lay ahead. So, I asked myself, on which birthday did having a social life become a mathematical challenge?

I confess I was the initiator of the first electronic communication that launched a seemingly endless string of emails, texts, and a few phone calls, in order to formulate a plan. In all fairness, I have to say that the woman I call "Lucy" had no idea that I was already in deep negotiations with "Ethel," and that my response to her had contingencies. And, while in this scenario I was able to keep it together, next time it might very well be me with a less-than-solid grasp of the days of the week.

So, in the spirit of "we have to laugh at ourselves or ingest antidepressants," I share with you the content of the communications that transpired over a four-day period. And if you, like me, were "booming" before the Boomers, I trust you will find this account highly relatable.

Also, in the spirit of "you can't make this stuff up," only the names have been changed (except mine) to protect the discombobulated.

Friday, June 7th, 12:13 PM
Email from Susan to Ethel
Hi: Hope you and Fred are well. I'm writing to see if we can make a date for dinner in the not-too-distant future, assuming your calendar isn't already booked for the summer. LOL

Sunday, June 9th, 8:25 PM
Email from Ethel to Susan
We are very free. How's next Friday night?

Monday, June 10th, 12:01 PM
Email from Susan to Ethel
Friday night is good, but not before 7:30. So if that's okay, we're on!

Monday, June 10th, 1:02 PM
Email from Ethel to Susan
Yes. Perfect! It's on the calendar.

Monday, June 10th, 1:16 PM
Email from Lucy to Susan
Any chance you're available this Saturday for dinner?

Monday, June 10th, 1:21 PM
Email from Susan to Lucy
Just made a date for Friday, but we are available Saturday. Would love to see you and Ricky.

Monday, June 10th, 3:06 PM
Email from Lucy to Susan
Perfect.

Monday, June 10th, 3:11 PM
Email from Ethel to Susan
I am so sorry. We have a conflict for Friday. Is Saturday good for you?

Monday, June 10th, 3:15 PM
Phone call from Susan to Ethel
Just made a plan for Saturday, but I will confirm to make sure my other friend didn't also double-book. LOL

Monday, June 10th, 3:30 PM
Phone call from Susan to Lucy
Just calling to make sure Saturday night plans are firm. Yes, they are? We're all set. Yes, I'll call the restaurant and make the reservation, no problem.

Monday, June 10th, 3:35 PM
Phone call from Susan to Ethel
Confirming that we can't do Saturday night, so let's reschedule. Busy on the 21st and 22nd. So, how's Saturday, the 29th. It's good? You sure? Yes. Okay, I'm writing it down. You write it down, too, please.

Monday, June 10, 3:41 PM
Email from Ethel to Susan
Can't do the 22nd, Saturday. Does Friday, the 21st work?

Monday, June 10, 3:46 PM
Email from Susan to Ethel
   We had agreed on Saturday, the 29th, not the 22nd. I can't do the 22nd either.

Monday, June 10, 3:50 PM
Email from Ethel to Susan
   Got it. You're right. Where is the nearest old age home?

Monday, June 10, 4:06 PM
Text from Lucy to Susan
   When I got home, I realized that Mildred had already invited us out for Saturday evening. Can we reschedule for the 28th or 29th of June?

Monday, June 10th, 5:13 PM
Email from Susan to Ethel
   You're not going to believe this. I just got a text from the person who wanted to see us this Saturday night saying she screwed up. Anyhow, we are now free and would love to reschedule. That's this Saturday, June 15th.

Tuesday, June 11th, 9:50 AM
Email from Ethel to Susan
   OMG! We cannot now. It's Tuesday at 10:00 AM and my brain is already scrambled. Let's start over. We, the Mertzes, are now free Friday night, but not Saturday.

Tuesday, June 11th, 10:42 AM
Email from Susan to Ethel
   We can go back to Friday and cancel the 29th. And don't worry. This is great material for a new blog!

Tuesday, June 11th, 11:00 AM
Text from Susan to Lucy
   Okay, worked out all the kinks. We can reschedule our dinner for the 29th. I carved it in stone.

Tuesday, June 11th, 11:30 AM
Text from Lucy to Susan
Stone seems a little rigid.

Tuesday, June 11, 1:00 PM
Email from Susan to Ethel
So, do we have a date for this Friday at 7:30? I hope so.

Tuesday, June 11, 1:01 PM
Email from Ethel to Susan
Yes!!!

Tuesday, June 11, 1:05 PM
Email from Susan to Ethel
Hallelujah!

Remarkably, when it was all over, we ended up with Fred and Ethel exactly where we began. And I'm pleased to relate that we all remembered to show up last night at the designated time and place and had a lovely evening. But I believe that, for the future, we must seek a better way to maintain our social calendars. Although I'm loath to bring up the health care debate, there is one solution for which I would lobby. That is, the expansion of Medicare benefits to include a secretary!

Notorious SBA

Raise your hand if you know that today is the birthday of Susan B. Anthony. As I thought. Only one hand raised, and it's mine. Or maybe there was one other hand raised somewhere in the back row. What a responsibility it has been all these years to be the only person in the room harboring this important piece of knowledge.

And how is it that I became the keeper of this factoid? The answer to this, and probably most of my other quirks, dates back, of course, to my childhood. And to savings banks. That's right, savings banks. In the days when savings banks looked like ancient marble mausoleums. And had higher interest rates. Additionally, if you walked into a bank in the 40s or 50s and opened a new account, you just might leave with a toaster or an electric wall clock.

Well, I must have grown up in the wrong neighborhood, because all our bank gave away was a paper calendar. Pathetic as this giveaway was, my mother brought the calendar home and hung it on a wall in our kitchen. And although the calendar could not brown your bread or tell the time, that's not to say it wasn't useful. Each day was represented by a little square where you could inscribe an appointment, or some other reminder. And the little square would also tell you if a particular day had a particular significance, like the Chinese New Year, or Mexican Flag Day, or when there would be a full moon.

My favorite page on the calendar was for the month of February. Little narcissist that I was, it was my favorite because it's the month in which I was born. The second week of February was just chock full of important days. February 12: Lincoln's birthday, February 13: my birthday (Well, that wasn't exactly printed on the calendar, but hand printed on it by me.), February 14: St. Valentine's Day. And, last but not least, February 15: Susan B. Anthony's birthday. That lineup made me so proud. I must be so special to be surrounded by all those important people! I confess that at the time I had no knowledge of Susan B. Anthony, but I figured she must be an important person to have her own square—and to share my name.

And, oh yes, the following week, on February 22, there was a square marking the birth of George Washington. (On today's calendar, Lincoln and Washington are no longer entitled to their own birthdays, but have been efficiently combined into President's Day, which typically falls on no one's date of birth, but ensures a three-day weekend.)

As I got older, I learned who Susan B. Anthony was, but sadly misunderstood what she represented. To my nine-year-old ear, she fought for women's suffrage, which made absolutely no sense to me at all. You can surely understand why. Also, that she was a "suffer jet," which in today's world, sounds like she played quarterback on a losing football team.

But as children we mishear lots of things, like "Elephants Gerald," the jazz singer, "Round John Virgin" who's mentioned in the song "Silent Night," and "youth in Asia," who, horribly, were being murdered.

But I'm happy to say that by the time I was old enough to vote, it had all sorted itself out. I developed a full appreciation of Susan B. Anthony's place in history and her personal importance to me as a woman living in 2019, beyond the fact that we share a name.

She was born February 15, 1820, into a large Quaker family who were social activists, and active in the anti-slavery movement. She became a teacher, and fought for equal pay for women, who were paid less than their male counterparts. Sound familiar? She recognized early on that if women were to have any power at all, they needed the right to vote.

In 1852, she joined with Elizabeth Cady Stanton in the Women's Rights Movement and dedicated the rest of her life to women's suffrage. (See, I got it right this time.) Women who supported the cause were called suffragettes. (Professional football didn't even start until 1892.) She never married, and traveled the country, campaigning for abolition of slavery and women's rights. Frederick Douglas became a good friend.

In November 1872 the Notorious SBA voted illegally in the US Presidential election and was arrested. She was found guilty by the judge and ordered to pay a fine of $100. She refused to pay and walked away. The trial increased her profile, and her ability to raise funds, enabling her to spread her message of supporting equal rights for women.

She died in New York in 1906. Fourteen years later, in 1920, women's right to vote was guaranteed by the Nineteenth Amendment.

End of history lesson. Hopefully, I've contributed to spreading the word about the importance of Susan B. Anthony. And going forward, I will no longer be the only person in the room who knows that her birthday is February 15th.

Sitting on my desk right now is a contemporary appointment book. Like the bank calendar in my mother's kitchen, each day is represented by a little square. Still listed on the February page are Mexican Flag Day, Chinese New Year, and St. Valentine's Day. Lincoln's and Washington's birthdays have been replaced by Presidents' Day. And Susan B. Anthony is notably absent. So, would you be so kind as to pencil it in? And while you're at it, although it's over, mark down mine as well.

Flipping Out

The other evening, I accidentally discovered a new link to my inner child. I lost my front tooth. Or, as my dentist exclaimed, "My dear, you have fractured your incisor." Call it what you will, I now have a gaping space in my mouth that is aligned with my left nostril, and completely visible when I talk, laugh, smile, or eat. None of which I had ever considered giving up, particularly the last one.

Rediscovering one's inner child is thought to be very therapeutic. But this path I do not recommend. My speech pattern has regressed to that of a lisping five-year-old, only a lot less adorable. And currently, biting into a bagel is simply out of the question.

Why this unfortunate incident occurred points to yet another aspect of my inner child. I was attempting to eat a Fudgsicle. Remember Fudgsicles? They were a dessert of choice long before there was such a thing as Häagen-Dazs, the ice cream with the fake Dutch name that was created in the Bronx and first sold in Brooklyn, or Ben and Jerry's, or all those fancy gelati now available in the freezer case of your local supermarket.

As a kid, the Fudgsicle—a chocolate spinoff of the popsicle—along with the creamsicle, were among my favorite treats. In those days I didn't worry about calories or sugar content. Now the Fudgsicles I purchase are artificially sweetened, mere shadows of their former selves.

Nevertheless, after dinner, I still look forward to my nostalgic goody. On the night in question, however, my first bite resulted in disaster.

Granted, Fudgsicles are frozen. But not quite as frozen as, let's say, an ice cube or a forgotten steak that's been sitting in the back of the freezer since last summer's barbecue. Having bitten into numerous Fudgsicles in the recent past, I hardly expected to pull back from this one with a loose tooth!

Fortunately, I made it to the dentist before the tooth actually deserted me. He looked at me, shook his head, laid a lead collar around my neck, and proceeded to take an X-ray. A few moments later he walked back into the room.

"I have bad news and worse news," he stated, "which would you like first?"

"Let me have the bad news first," I replied, "then we can build up to the other. I've always been a big fan of crescendos."

"Well, I thought we could get away with a crown," he declared. "But the tooth is too far gone for that."

"And the worse news?"

"I will have to extract the tooth"

"And then?" I queried.

"You are going to need an implant."

And that was the moment the cymbals crashed!

Now, implants aren't so bad, although they do make a considerable dent in one's bank account. I'm a proud owner of several already. But due to its location, this one was horrifying. Between the time the implant was inserted and the months it took to heal, I would look like an extra from *The Beverly Hillbillies.*

The answer to this humiliating situation, my dentist explained, was something called a "Flipper."

"I'll take two," I responded with a mixture of panic and relief. He assured me that one would suffice.

So, what was left of my front tooth was yanked out, and too crumbled to even consider putting under my pillow. (My inner child still believed in the Tooth Fairy.) And to assuage my dignity, I was presented with "The Flipper."

This custom-made piece of plastic, on which hangs a replica on my missing tooth, has become my best new frenemy. While it allows me to smile without humiliation, it is about as comfortable as a tongue depressor. Once inserted, it feels like someone has attached a shelf to my upper palate.

If I happen to see you in the near future, and we engage in conversational pleasantries, let me assure you that I am not inebriated. I only sound sloshed due to my friend Flipper, which is giving my poor tongue a very hard time when it comes to producing "s" sounds. As a result, I'm avoiding meeting new people. I'm reluctant to say my name.

Dining is no joy either. I don't wear the damn thing when I'm home, but since recreational eating is part of the Florida lifestyle, I don't dare go into a restaurant without my new companion. Perhaps we've discovered the Flipper diet!

I do have a choice. I can choose not to wear it at all and tell people that I'm auditioning for a role in the remake of the movie *Deliverance.* Or I can toss vanity to the wind, and grin and bear it. Well, maybe not a full grin, perhaps just a closed-mouth little smirk.

Or better yet, there is an option for a temporary tooth to be bonded in place. If that happens, I will happily lock Flipper inside its case and banish it to the back of some drawer.

But for now, I will tolerate my annoying device, since going toothless is not a coveted fashion statement. And, most important, I'm sure it will be an asset when I bite into my next Fudgsicle.

An Uplifting Experience

Ladies, did you know that when you walk into a store to buy a new bra, the odds are that you're going to buy the wrong size? And, if you've been buying bras for as long as I have, this is very disturbing news. Now I stay awake at night, wondering how improper bra selection has affected my life.

What triggered this most recent insomnia episode was an article I read in last Thursday's *The New York Times* about the ignorant and uninformed way we unsuspecting women go about making choices about our undergarments. Who knew such a topic would be worthy of an entire page? Right up there with world peace, global warming, immigration, hacked emails, and a shortage of clean drinking water.

While I do spend a considerable amount of time fretting about all those issues, this new concern really hit home. It's up close and very personal. And directly impacts my life on a daily basis. How could I not have known, after all these years, that I might be a victim of Ill-Fitting Bra Syndrome (or, as it's known in the medical community, "IBS," which, unfortunately is frequently confused with Irritable Bowel Syndrome, the other IBS, which receives a lot more attention).

And, of course, it was a man, a plastic surgeon, who pointed (no pun intended) this out. He mansplained that 70% of women were wearing the wrong size bra and suggested a revolutionary method for measuring breasts. Unfortunately, the article did not report on the specifics of his theory on boob sizing.

In any event, his focus seems to have triggered an entire scientific field of study on the upper female anatomy and the garments which contain them. Not just here in America, but by our friends across the pond, as well. One such study cited in *The Times* article was entitled "Evaluation of Professional Bra Fitting Criteria for Bra Selection and Fitting in the U.K." This title brought two questions to mind: 1) who the heck would fund such a study; and, more important, 2) are British breasts different from my own? The author of said study was quoted as saying "there aren't many scientific papers which have effectively looked at issues of bra fit…" Gee, I wonder why not?

Who took you shopping for your first bra? It was your mother, no doubt. And how did she ever manage to be helpful without a degree in anatomy and physiology? At the time, if you were like me, you were probably barely out of an undershirt, so any triple A with straps and hooks would satisfy the emerging pubescent female anatomy.

According to this article, when it comes to understanding the biomechanics of the perfect fit, I have been an abject failure. Until now, I knew nothing of bands, straps, gores, the precise placement of underwires, something called "breast volume," or the proper "scoop and swoop" technique of fitting one's boob into the cup. How ill-prepared I've been all these years. It's no wonder that I've never been good at sports, have illegible handwriting, and suck at math!

And men, just so you don't feel left out of this discussion, think of what it would be like to have to shop for the perfect jock strap!

But there was also salvation contained in the printed word. The article went on to assure me that if my bra doesn't fit right, it was not my fault. It appears that there is a lack of an industry standard. Shame on you, Victoria's Secret, Hanes, Maidenform, Playtex! A 34C for one should be a 34C for all!

Fortunately, after all the decades spent in lingerie fitting rooms, I think I've found the undergarment that, while perhaps not ideal, works best for me. So, thank you very much, I will pass on the blogs, YouTube videos, charts, and guidelines, all designed to assist me with my next purchase.

And although I've made peace with my IBS, and am grateful for all my good fortune, I can't help but wonder how much better my life would have been if only I had found the perfect bra!

Hot Town, Summer in the City

This summer, I was fortunate enough to be able to spend more time than usual in the Big Apple. I realize that, based on what I just related, some of you might believe that the heat got to me and altered any semblance of rational thinking. But, hey, I'm a city kid, born and bred. And although I've spent the last few decades where the grass grows, somehow the sound of jack hammers remains more familiar than lawn mowers.

Part of my urban daily routine, besides familiarizing my suburban dog with concrete, is walking and gawking. A word about walking, before I get to the gawking part: I have happily rediscovered putting one foot in front of the other as a means of transportation! Walking is no longer limited to the treadmill or getting to and from my car in the mall parking lot, but as an actual means of reaching a destination without wheels.

As far as gawking is concerned, as a non-reader of fashion magazines or The New York Times Styles section, there is no place like a big city to discover the current trends in female apparel. The sidewalks are a veritable runway, with scores of young women reflecting what's hip.

There was plenty of skin to be seen this summer. Miniskirts made a big comeback, as well as shirts with mostly empty buttonholes. Fashion was ripped from the courts, as cute little pleated tennis skirts became streetwear. And workout bras were not limited to the gym.

One trend that did surprise me, however, was shorts with loafers…and socks. Had some millennial visited their grandpa in Boca and decided that this was a good look?

But most of all, I think I will remember the summer of 2021 as the season of the belly button. The hottest look of all in these months of hotness was extreme crop tops accompanied by bottoms that rested just below the navel. Whether the bottoms be short skirts or baggy cargo pants, exposed midriffs were all the rage. It was flesh running rampant after a year of Covid-related seclusion.

Torsos were everywhere. During my walks, I stopped noticing the faces of the young women coming towards me but became an unwilling observer of stomachs. Was all that exposed skin meant to be stared at? If so, I was certainly doing my share.

At some point, this whole phenomenon became a bit unnerving, and I found myself indulging in a bit of fantasy. What if I were a witness to an accident, or a crime, and was questioned by a detective?

"You say you saw the whole incident?" he would state. "So what color was her hair?"

"Sorry, sir, I never noticed her hair. But I can say with certainty that she was definitely an outie."

But, back to reality. Something else I noticed with pleasant surprise was that this nakedness was not limited to women with super flat tummies, although there were plenty of those. Even fuller-figured women with a bit of "spillage" had the confidence to step outside and bare their middles. Raise a glass to "body positivity!"

And speaking of body positivity, you might have noticed that in this essay, I tended to repeat the adjective "young" as I discussed these partially dressed women. As an experienced Medicare recipient, was I just a wee bit envious of their courage? Did I wish myself young again, strutting along the sidewalk without any concern about exposing love handles?

I'm reminded of being on a beach in France, where topless bathing was the rule rather than the exception. And age did not prevent the older woman from letting it all hang out, sometimes literally. But the women were free, and no one paid it any mind.

So, should there be an age limit on wearing crop tops? I'll let you decide for yourself. As for me, I relinquish crop tops, along with those jeans that look like they've been through a paper shredder, to those who have no idea who Julius La Rosa was. I'm keeping my Buddha belly safely tucked away and invite passersby to focus on one of my more flattering features. Like, say, the super cute dog who is trotting by my side.

My Life as a Car

I'm not sure if I really believe in reincarnation, but I do find the notion very seductive. One can take a measure of comfort in the belief that, although one's physical body may be dead, the soul can still thrive. Just think about it. I, or at least my soul, can start a new life in a different physical body or form. Which leads me to ponder about my present life, and whether my existence as Susan just may have been the result of transmigration, and in a former life I was, let's say, a platypus. But a discussion about past lives is a topic for another day.

If you're wondering what triggered consideration of reincarnation at this time, I'm about to tell you. (Even if you're not wondering, I'm about to tell you.) You can blame it on the time of year. It's fall, all right, but for me, it's also check-up season. It's the time when all my annual medical visits come due, and with each passing year, it seems the calendar of appointments grows longer, and I am running from one doctor's office to the next. My body is no longer a singular entity, but is dissected into its separate components, each one falling under the purview of a different medical specialist.

So, what does this have to do with reincarnation, you may well ask? (Even if you don't ask, I'm about to tell you.) Assuming I have some personal input as to where my soul lands in the next life, I've decided that I want to return as a car. And although I'm still trying to decide about make and model, foreign or domestic, sexy or practical, I'm certain that I want to spend my next go-around on earth as an automobile.

Does my choice surprise you? (Even if it doesn't, I'm about to explain.) It's simple, really. At least to me. Since Labor Day I have visited an ophthalmologist, cardiologist, gastroenterologist (that was the worst) periodontist, radiologist, and gynecologist. Waiting in the wings are the dermatologist, podiatrist, internist, and at least one more, whose specialty escapes me at the moment. (Perhaps it's a memory doctor?) It's exhausting!

But when I'm a car, and it's time for my routine checkups, will I have to make numerous appointments and drive around from waiting room to waiting room? No! It can all be accomplished in a single visit at one location.

While I'll continue to have as many moving parts as I currently do, possibly more, I will not be required to make separate appointments with a transmission expert, or a tire-rotation specialist. I will not need someone with a degree in oil changes, brake examination, or piston inspection, not to mention a lube maven.

And, the visit won't require my insurance cards, photo id, or checking off the boxes on an endless number of forms inquiring about my medical history. And the mechanic is not interested in the number of pills I take, or if there's any possibility that I might be pregnant.

And best of all, I will no longer be required to wear those ridiculous paper gowns that open in the front (or is it the back?), that barely cover your anatomy no matter where you tie the strings.

When I'm a new car, the maintenance visits will be simple. But as I get older, and some of my parts need replacing, there won't be the hassle about finding the right specialist. The same friendly mechanic will have me up and running in no time.

All things considered, I think I've made a rational choice for my next life. And I feel supported by the fact that, if one examines the word "reincarnation" they will surely find the clue that helped guide me in this direction.

And when my mileage adds up, and it's my time for a trade-in, I won't be sad. Instead, I will focus on the possibilities for my next life. Perhaps I can be something without a body altogether and be completely maintenance-free. So, if I do have a choice, next time I should like to be Alexa.

My Baby Needs Bifocals? That's Not Right

I have, over time, come to accept the fact that I am an old person. Chronologically, anyway. Although like most of my peers, I find it difficult to reconcile the woman who lives inside my head with the one who was just offered a seat on the bus by a chivalrous young man. Nevertheless, realist that I am, I can't pretend that the world at large does not notice my gray hair, chicly cut though it is, my collagen deficits, or my sensible shoes in place of stilettos.

I've made peace with the irregular blip on my EKG, and the fact that I now need medication. I've made peace with the need for certain body part replacements, and the fact that my eyesight ain't what it was. All that, as well as the other indignities that come with another candle on the cake. (Hearing's still okay, but we're taking it one day at a time.)

But there is one other aspect of aging that I have yet to reconcile. It's the realization that my own children, my babies, are now middle-aged, and in many respects, have caught up with me. What was I doing when their hair started to gray?

The other day, I was speaking on the phone with my youngest, who is about to turn fifty. We chatted about, amongst other things, his recent eye exam.

"Is everything okay?" I asked hesitantly.

"Yes," he assured me, everything was fine except that his vision had worsened.

And, suddenly, we were discussing the benefits of progressive lenses over bifocals.

Bifocals? That, along with hearing aids, I had always regarded as an old-person's accessory. How could it be that my baby needs bifocals? If he's old enough for bifocals, where does that put me? Somewhere up there with Mrs. Methuselah?

Reflecting back ten years or so, I can now recall seeing the first specks of gray in my older son's hair. That is, before his hairline began to recede and he started wearing his 'do closer to the scalp. Come to think of it, the specks were noticeable in my younger son's as well. Was that before or after he informed me that his cholesterol was borderline, and the doctor had prescribed a statin?

Along with these shared signs of aging, it is absolutely startling to recognize that our middle-aged children and we, their parents, have actually become part of the same demographic. The evidence is everywhere.

This summer my "baby" will most likely receive a birthday notice from AARP, along with an invitation to join. If he does so, he and I will be entitled to the same senior discounts and carry matching membership cards in our respective wallets. In a few years, if I decide to move to one of those 55+ adult communities, I won't have to sneak him in in the trunk of my car. In fact, he could run for president of the co-op board without faking his ID. And just last night I saw an ad on

TV that was attempting to convince seniors to purchase life insurance. Did I hear correctly when the announcer claimed to be talking to anyone between the ages of fifty and eighty-five? As I noted above, my ears are still very much in working order.

I write for a publication called *Lifestyles After 50*. Along with my cohorts, all our adult children will soon be eligible for their subscription list. (Some already are.) And personally, I belong to an organization for professional women aged fifty and over. While this excludes the males, the three daughters are more than welcome to join. We can carpool to the meetings.

And what might be the most fun? If we all enroll in the continuing education seminar entitled Love, Dating, and Sex Over 50, we can carpool to that one as well.

So, dear Gen X children, for better or worse, you have collided with both the Baby Boomers and us, the Silent Generation. Welcome.

A few years ago, I wrote a piece about my two Labrador retrievers, Bette and Davis, who lived with us from eight weeks old to sixteen years. In fact, the title of the essay became the title of my first book, *How Old Am I* in Dog Years? They were thirteen and fourteen when I wrote the essay, and my point was the many ways our puppies had caught up with us when one considered arthritis and hearing loss. Who would have thought that I would return to the same place, once again pondering the curiosities of life, and how in hell I got to where *my own baby* could possibly need bifocals?

Old Dog, New Tricks

I'm pleased to state that when it comes to technology, I have one foot and two and a half toes in the twenty-first century! Reluctant as I was at first to embrace this brave new world, I did eventually relinquish my electric typewriter.

And, while I may have been the last kid on the block to finally purchase a smart phone, I must admit that I'm now as hooked as the rest of the population who never watch where they're walking.

I confess I didn't jump in all at once, but proceeded slowly, on a need-to-know basis. Hey, but look at me now! I Skype, I text, I Zoom. I participate in webinars and online meetings. I stream, I message, I email, and I'm a whiz with attachments. I own an iPad and Google and Amazon are my best friends. My websites confirm that my passwords are powerful! Content with the status quo, I do tend to shy away from updates.

I've mastered the meaning of pdf and MP3 and know that Adobe does not necessarily refer to Native American homes in the southwest. I create files and folders, store photos, type documents, scan, print, fax, spread sheet, Facebook, tweet, and a whole lot more. (I realize I'm starting to sound like the actor in the UPS Store commercial. Forgive me.)

And, as the family bookkeeper, I've mastered a multi-faceted bookkeeping program, which I've been using for over ten years.

So why, with a resume like mine, did I break out in hives when our new accountant suggested that I consider switching to a different method for keeping track of our finances?

He claimed this new program had many advantages over the old, and in time, I would learn to love it. In time? How much time? But there was no wriggling out of this proposal after he offered to come to my home and give me a tutorial. So, we set a date.

I realized that my equilibrium was in serious jeopardy because for five consecutive nights before the appointed time, I awoke at three with a recurring nightmare. In my dream, it was always the tenth of the month. I was sitting at the computer, using the new program to pay our bills. As I attempted to enter the dollar amount, a scrawny hand with long, pointy fingernails reached out from behind me and added additional zeros to my figure. Before I could stop it, the hand pressed the "enter" key. This occurred again and again while the creature with the scrawny hand vocalized his evil cackle. I was powerless. Soon all our bank accounts were empty, and we were forced to live in our car. And while we were gathering our meager belongings, the dog claimed the back seat.

In truth, I was nervous about the transition from the old to the new and had real daytime visions of doing something awful that would eliminate ten years of impeccable record-keeping. The impending visit by the accountant loomed large, and in my quivering mind he became a preying, fearful figure, replete with black cloak.

Did I need any more proof that I was overreacting? Would anyone with a functional IQ actually be afraid of an accountant? To calm my nerves, I promised to reward myself with that expensive blouse I had admired at the local boutique.

Fast-forward to the day of the visit. He showed up right on time, looking quite normal in casual Wednesday business attire. He sat next to me in front of my computer, close enough for me to discern that there were no fangs where his canines should be. Step-by-step, he led me through the functions of this new-and-improved method for recording our financial transactions. By step three I could sense my blood pressure beginning to lower.

It took a few hours, but under his tutelage, I was moving out of my comfort zone, and manipulating transactions like it was part of my DNA. I confess that I did panic a bit when he started packing up to leave, refusing my offer of dinner and a place to sleep. But I opened the program the next day all on my own, and guess what? I was fine. And so, I bought the blouse.

So, what's the take-away from all of this? Don't let another birthday rob you of your confidence. It is a challenge to learn something new when you've been used to the same old thing for a long time. But an old dog *can* learn a new trick. Provided the bone comes with a substantial price tag!

Group Membership

I reached a milestone birthday this past weekend. No parades, no fireworks, and I respectfully social-distanced with my friends by not inviting them to a party. Instead, I passed a quiet evening with my honey at our favorite Italian restaurant, outside of course. And no gifts, please. I live in Florida now and have no need for any more scarves.

But now that I've crossed over into a new decade, I couldn't help but wonder where exactly I landed on the aging spectrum. As many of you know, my chosen career path as a clinical speech pathologist was working with an "elderly" population. As a young middle-aged professional, I studied the field of aging and learned from the social scientists, gerontologists I believed they're called, about the arc of aging. They wrote about the "young old" and the "old old," and the boundary between the two being defined by your last birthday.

Well, given that I was now four-score, that certainly was a sobering concept! And, while I'm still able to propel myself out of bed each morning, I was not going to take this lying down. Surely by now, with the ever-increasing life span, I suspected the parameters for what is old age must have shifted. And I was correct.

To demonstrate that my essays are not merely irrelevant, but also educational, I am about to share with you the latest studies defining sub-groups of the aging process. I discovered several hypotheses. To be perfectly honest, I rejected the study that defined "very old" as 80+. Instead, in the interest of staving off the inevitable, the following results were more to my liking: Young Old: 65-74, Middle Old: 75-84, and Old Old: 85+. (Sorry, honey, maybe you want to skip your next birthday.)

But if you, like I am, are an adherent of the "age is just a number" principal, you reject the notion of categorization based on chronology. Instead, you believe that functionality should be the guidepost. With that goal in mind, I present you with the following checklist. Rating yourself in the following categories should result in a more accurate representation of your true standing among the hyphenated numerical groupings stated above. Please respond honestly.

1. Number of times you awaken to pee:
   a. 0
   b. 1 – 2
   c. You're too tired in the morning to remember

2. When putting on your underwear you can:
   a. Balance on one foot
   b. Balance on one foot but gently touch the adjacent wall
   c. Sit on the edge of the bed—gave up balancing years ago

3. When a light bulb burns out in an overhead light, you feel safe:
   a. Standing on a two-step ladder
   b. Standing on a one-step ladder
   c. Calling the handyman

4. Regarding driving, you:
   a. Still drive at night
   b. Ask your spouse to drive at night
   c. Call an Uber

5. Regarding alcohol consumption, you:
   a. Can still handle a scotch, neat, without making a fool of yourself
   b. Used to handle a scotch, neat, but now request it with ice
   c. Pretend to order a scotch, then secretly ask the waiter for a Diet Coke in a rocks glass

6. Hearing:
   a. The volume of the TV does not drive your spouse from the room
   b. The volume of the TV does drive your spouse from the room
   c. The volume of the TV causes your neighbor to call the police

7. For Women:
   a. You can still hook your bra behind your back
   b. You can only hook your bra in the front then twist it around to the back
   c. You've given up wearing a bra altogether

8. Strength
   a. You can get up from the couch in one try
   b. You can get up from the couch in two tries
   c. You claim the couch is quite comfortable and decide to sleep there

9. Your offspring
   a. are beginning to look middle age
   b. are middle age
   c. are now eligible to live in the same adult community as you do

10. Memory
    a. You remember what you ate for breakfast yesterday
    b. You remember what you ate for breakfast this morning
    c. What's breakfast?

I hope you found these ten categories helpful in determining your standing in this third stage of life. But if your honest answers were mostly "Cs," don't despair. You're not alone. As the wise man said, "Remember, inside every older person there's a younger person wondering what the hell happened!"

Utter Nonsense

Yeet! Get ready Boomers and Pre-Boomers, it's Spring Break time again and your Gen Z grandkids are on the loose. Want to spend some time with them and be really savage? Then don't be a baby and learn to talk the talk!

Yes, it's time for our annual English as a Second Language quiz. Challenge your brain with these ten examples of the latest Gen Z code words. Your results will predict whether intergenerational conversation is still possible.

1. Lewk
    a. Not too hot and not too cold
    b. A comedian that almost made it
    c. A misspelling by a dyslexic plumber
    d. A, maybe B

2. Dank
   a. Past tense of dink
   b. Abbreviated German "thank you"
   c. If you think it means musty and damp, you're cold!
   d. A or C, but never B

3. Finna
   a. A Mark Twain book translated into Italian
   b. Someone refusing a $5 bill
   c. The end of "na"
   d. None of the above

4. LMIRL
   a. A lonely vowel surrounded by four consonants
   b. A new classification system for preferred sexual orientation
   c. A failed effort to bring back Lucky Strike cigarettes
   d. B, definitely B!

5. Stan
   a. Ollie's friend
   b. Nats spelled backward
   c. The short form of Borat's native land
   d. Who cares?

6. Finsta
   a. A Scandinavian unmarried woman
   b. A typo of "finna"
   c. A new French cheese
   d. All of the above

7. Wojak
   a. Telly Savalas' Polish cousin
   b. A man named Jacob with lots of tsuris
   c. Trying to stop a horse named Jack
   d. Are you kidding me?

8. Mittens
   a. Something to warm your hands. Not!
   b. One more than nine baseball gloves
   c. The result of crossing mice with baby cats
   d. Some of the above

9. Bet
   a. The second letter of the Hebrew alphabet
   b. Short form of Midler's first name
   c. Short form of Davis' first name
   d. Are we there yet?

10. Cap/No Cap
    a. Do I need a yarmulke in a Reform synagogue?
    b. An upper- or lower-case letter is optional
    c. Dilemma over best way to repair a broken tooth
    d. I'm getting a migraine!

What the scores mean: Excellent, 7 to 10 points (You are Savage), Pretty Good, 4 to 6 points (No Cap), You are sleeping on, 0 to 3 points.

What the slang words or phrases really mean: Lewk: something that's your personal signature style, Dank: excellent or very high quality, Finna: I am going to…, LMIRL: let's meet in real life, Stan: an obsessive fan, but not a creepy one, Finsta: secret social media account, Wojak: An internet meme used to express emotion, Mittens: something not quite amazing, Bet: a sarcastic "no," Cap/No Cap: Lying/ not lying, Savage: someone or something that is really great or cool, Sleeping on: not paying enough attention to someone or something.

The Thrill of the Shill

May is Older Americans Month, or so proclaimed President Gerald Ford in 1976. It's the month that the nation is supposed to honor all the past and present contributions made by its senior citizens. Since I've already wasted fifteen days in not acknowledging the greatness of my cohorts, I thought I'd use this essay to pay tribute to a particular segment of my generation—the Senior Grifter, or stated in a friendlier way, the Senior Influencer.

Yes, it appears that my age group has discovered Instagram. Ergo, becoming an "influencer" on social media is no longer just a young person's game. Older adults, particularly women, have discovered that age is not a barrier to people with no particular talent being able to acquire thousands and thousands of followers. All you need is a gimmick and the willingness to sometimes make a fool of yourself. And, oh yes, the ability to convince people that if they do what you tell them to do, then their life can be as wonderful as yours.

In case you've been asleep, let me give you some examples. Notorious among the younger influencers is the Kardashian/ Jenner clan. Can they sing? Do they tap dance, act, or even play the ukulele? No. None of the above. And yet, they have been wildly successful at marketing themselves as lifestyle gurus, and beauty experts. They get paid millions for endorsing products to millions of gullible followers.

Wait. What? You mean to say you haven't heard of Huda Kattan, Jeffree Star, Jordan Lipscome, or Sophia & Cinzia, whose charmed lives are all about fashion, travel, fitness, and promoting gorgeous while looking absurd? And just a side note: a particular travel influencer got caught "not really being there!" So much for authenticity.

You can watch their videos on your own time. Right now, I want to turn to the real honorees of my current essay—the older folks who have been labeled the "Granfluencers."

What better place to begin than with ninety-two-year-old Helen Ruth Elam, known as Baddiewinkle on her platform. For ten years, she's been looking absolutely ridiculous in flamboyant feather boas, overly large shades, and skimpy red dresses. But hey, who am I to judge? She's laughing all the way to the bank with sponsorships from Amazon, Canada Dry, LG, and Svedka Vodka. But who the hell are her over three million followers, and why? I pose the same question for the rest of this list.

Then there's sixty-eight-year-old Lyn Slater, who, to her credit, become an accidental icon because she was caught dressing, not ridiculously, but fashionably. So, hey, why not give up your teaching job, wear ripped jeans, and make social influencing your career?

And how about a shout-out for seventy-three-year-old Jenny Kee whose requisite oversized eyeglasses, shaved hair style, and mismatched prints have earned her the spotlight in Instagram stardom?

Let's not forget the gorgeous Grece Ghanem with her plunging necklines.

And, last but not least, there is Joan MacDonald, who actually has something to offer. Rather than flaunting glitz and glamour, Joan, at the age of seventy-five, is an exercise guru. Her Instagram exercise videos have more than 35,000 likes. She'll lead you through a tough workout, and at the end, while you're panting, she'll casually mention the manufacturer of the outfit she's wearing. You go girl!

Let's face it. Celebrity has always been used to sell. Actors and sports figures get paid to endorse products all the time and have been doing so forever. But the rise of social media marketing has certainly broadened the playing field—so many "young" hopefuls taking selfies in the hope of becoming a media star.

So, during this Older Americans month, kudos to the golden girls who got in on the game. Grifting should not be wasted on the young!

Want to Add Years to Your Life? Try Complaining

What a great time to be a professional complainer. Like myself. And to have written a how-to book about the subject, which will, no doubt, be catapulted to the best seller list due to a recent article in *The New York Times*.

Nearly ten years into my third-act career I have finally been validated. Rather than making one feel like a pariah, complaining has now been elevated to a position of social positivity, standing shoulder to shoulder with other acceptable acts such as bathing and coughing into one's elbow. Besides, to quote from the article, "expressing negative feelings is actually healthy." And who amongst us does not rejoice in a sense of well-being?

But hold on. Before you jump on the grousing bandwagon, according to the article, there's a right way and a wrong way to complain. And starting off on the wrong foot will just screw up your efforts and give you something else to complain about. Which may or may not be a bad thing.

When I began writing and kvetching about things like the inequality that exists in choosing select cities for the release of new movies, little did I know that in a parallel universe, social scientists were actually conducting serious investigations into something that came as naturally to me as breathing. And the results were the substance of the previously mentioned article.

However, as I read through said article, doubts infiltrated my comfort zone. Was my complaining constructive, or was I merely ruminating and catastrophizing, both of which are serious no-nos for professional complainers. According to the experts, if you ruminate or catastrophize, you can become depressed. And if you're feeling hopeless, why bother complaining? So naturally, my aspiration was to be constructive.

Other questions began haunting me as well. For example, how was my complaining impacting others? Was I frustrating my confidantes or bonding with my readers? Perhaps I needed to develop a brief survey to get to the bottom of this. On the other hand, did I really want to know?

Instead of the survey, I turned to the author of a book called *Constructive Wallowing* (wish I had come up with that one!) who reminded me that I was using complaining as a social tool. I'm not sure what that meant exactly, but I did feel a bit of comfort.

I was also relieved to learn that complaining was a powerful stress reliever. And we all know the toll that stress can take, particularly in the express-checkout line in the supermarket. So, if I vent about the person in front of me who has seventeen items in their cart rather than the requisite twelve, it could add years to my life.

And speaking of venting, the article states that "when done effectively, it can help you clearly realize what, specifically, about a situation is bothering you." But sadly, it neglects to provide any criteria for venting effectiveness. If I'm going to spend time and energy blowing off steam, I surely want to get the best result!

Another important lesson gleaned from the article was that the most beneficial type of complaining, in terms of your health and relationships, was to be sure it was "strategic." Again, not being exactly certain about what went into a strategic complaint as opposed to a haphazard one, I surmised that it had something to do with your desired outcome.

For example, is your goal to vent, problem solve, or ruminate? By now, we've learned that ruminating can be hazardous to your health, so let's skip right over that one. Which leaves venting or problem solving. It isn't clear to me whether you can claim both as a desired outcome. In a perfect world, this should definitely be an option. But we know the world is not perfect, which is why we complain in the first place.

So, if I follow the guidelines laid out above, my complaining will be productive. But if it's productive, will I have anything to complain about? Therein lies the conundrum.

So, folks, go ahead. Let it all out. It might even lower your cholesterol. And if you suffer from FOMO (fear of missing out) because you think your life is perfect, consider purchasing a copy of my second book, *How to Complain When There's Nothing to Complain About.* It will provide all the fodder you need for a hearty professional grumble!

Girls' Night Out: An Almost-True Story

I recently read a study that said fun is more fun when it's shared with friends. While this may be something we know instinctively, scientific validation is always reassuring. Now, when someone in your group asks, "Are we having fun yet?" you can roll your eyes and point to the data.

Thus, it was the seduction of fun times four that motivated me to contact my three BFFs and suggest a Girls' Night Out. That, plus the fact that I would soon be gone for seven months and not have the pleasure of their companionship.

One would think that at this stage of our lives, with fewer demands on our time, finding a single evening when the four of us might be free would not be difficult. Well, if one would think that, one would be dead wrong!

Instead, what ensued was a chain of emails filled with very complicated negotiations that did finally result in, not only a date night, but peace in the Middle East.

I share with you a small portion of the experience. Only the names have been changed to protect the not-so-innocent.

And there may be just a slight adjustment of the actual facts.

To: Meg@abc.com, Jo@def.net, Beth@omg.org
From: Amy@tmi.dot
Subject: Girls' Night Out
Hi, my three best friends. It's been too long since we've been together. How about planning an evening, just the four of us, before I fly south for the winter?

From: Beth@omg.org
Subject: Girls' Night Out
Great idea! Let's do it!

From: Meg@abc.com
Subject: GNO
Count me in! We always have such a blast. Why do we wait so long? We need to make this more of a priority in our lives.

From: Jo@def.net
Subject: GNO
Was thinking the same thing myself.

From: Amy@tmi.dot
Subject: GNO
Great! So, let's set a date.

From: Meg@abc.com
Subject: Setting a date
Rest of this month not looking good for me. Have Book Club, Cousins' Club, Bridge Club, and I might need root canal.

From: Amy@tmi.dot
Subject: Setting a date
Okay, let's look at next month then. I'll still be here, and dates are pretty open.

From: Jo@def.net:
Subject: Setting a date
Next month is good, except for the second Tuesday, fourth Friday, and forget Saturdays. And on the 4th, I need to prepare for a colonoscopy.

From: Beth@omg.org
Subject: Setting a date
I have a tentative business meeting on either the 5th or the 8th so I need to leave those dates open. And my daughter may be flying in on the 11th and staying until the 15th—not sure, but need to keep that open, as well.

From: Amy@tmi.dot
Subject: Setting a date
Still have 18 possibilities. Let's wait to hear from Meg.

From: Amy@tmi.dot
Subject: Setting a date
It's been four days since our last email. Anyone hear from Meg?

From: Amy@tmi.dot
Subject: Meg
Did Meg leave the country?

From: Meg@abc.com
Subject: Setting a date
Sorry for the delay, guys. Doesn't mean this isn't a priority.
  Let's see. I'm already double-booked for Wednesdays, so how about the first Tuesday or any Sunday?

From: Jo@def.net
Subject: Setting a date
Not Sundays! It's the final season of Homeland.

From: Beth@omg.org
Subject: Are you lame?
Haven't you heard about DVR-ing?

From: Jo@def.net
Subject: Homeland
It's not the same!

From: Amy@tmi.dot
Subject: Back to Setting a Date
Surely there must be one night in the entire month when we're all free!

From: Jo@def.com
Subject: GNO
If I change the date of my colonoscopy from 17th to the 23rd, and skip my ukulele class, that could free up next Tuesday.

From: Meg@abc.com
Subject: Next Tuesday
Maybe. Not sure. Must check with Harry.

From: Jo@def.net
Subject: Next Tuesday.
Who's Harry?

From: Meg@abc.com
Subject: Next Tuesday
He teaches Yoga and does privates on Tuesday night.

From: Amy@tmi.dot
Subject: Setting a Date. Not!
Well, guys, I think that does it for this year. And I'll be gone half of next year as well.

From: Meg@abc.com
Subject: Next year
And I'll be gone for the rest of the year.

From: Amy@tmi.dot
Subject: Setting a Date
So, how's 2023 looking so far?

Okay, so I exaggerated. Fact is, it wasn't easy, but we did finally set a date. And it's coming up soon. I have my fingers crossed that Harry can be flexible, the ukulele class gets cancelled, and no one has an unexpected visit from a third cousin. Would hate to go back to the table for more negotiations. But who knows? Perhaps in the next round we could also settle North Korea.

The Perfect Dress

I have been on a quest for the perfect dress. Perfect for me, that is. And I do have some very specific requirements. Requirements that I probably didn't have when I was 30 years younger. But you know how that is. If you don't know, you might be too young to relate to this essay. Or possibly the rare male who subscribes to my blog. In either case, there might not be anything in it for you, so continue at your own discretion.

The dress I'm seeking is not a dress for any special occasion. Just a casual dress suitable for warm summer weather, a dress I can wear to Stop and Shop, and then easily transition to an informal evening at the Shake Shack.

It's not that I have nothing to wear. My closet is far from empty. But I don't own a dress. And I'd really like to have one. I'm not a fashionista, but I have noticed that dresses are very popular this summer. I see them everywhere. And the women who wear them seem so fashionably summery, even when they're picking up poop in the dog park. Whereas my dog park attire, while functional, might also be appropriate for boot camp.

I have glanced into the many clothing stores in my small town and noted that they are crammed with dresses. I took that as a hopeful sign. Surely there would be one that was just right for me.

But, as noted above, I do have some very specific requirements. First, the dress must be collarless. I have a thing about collars. I don't like them. On me. On some women, collars look fine. But on me, they look like the top half of a parochial school uniform. All that's missing is the plaid, pleated skirt.

Sleeves, or lack thereof, is another matter. Sleeves didn't used to matter, but a few birthdays ago I decided that my ability to look attractive in sleeveless or stringy straps had reached its expiration date. So, my preference for sleeves these days is longish, even though it's summer. And if not long, no less than precisely three inches above the elbow. (I've decided to ignore any issues surrounding my elbows. I can't see them anyway.)

The length of my perfect dress is definitely below the knee, but ideally, it should reach the ankle. Both of them. While my legs remain one or two of my more attractive features, I prefer to leave the display of knees to women whose ages do not exceed the speed limit on most U.S. highways.

I am also particular about the shape of the dress. I require a loose, rather than fitted, silhouette. I believe in fashion jargon, that style is called "unconstructed." And that's the perfect look for me. My frame is no longer suitable as a construction site.

Flounces, ruffles, and bows are definitely no-nos. I am drawn to a more tailored, grown-up look. I have in the past tried on garments with frilly, full skirts. While looking adorable on a certain type, what the mirror reflected back to me was reminiscent of a beautifully wrapped gift box of fine chocolates. But Godiva was not the look I was seeking. Obviously, she couldn't find a suitable dress either!

I know it's summer, and florals are all the rage. But my preference is not to look like something ordered from 1-800-Flowers. Therefore, I require a dress in a summery, but solid color, or a pattern that doesn't look like it's trying to be heard in a noisy restaurant. I'm not fussy about the fabric. As long as it's soft and cool. And not see-through. Or clingy. Or becomes wrinkled if you even look at it the wrong way.

Sadly, I have not yet found the perfect dress. I'm not sure why. I don't think my requirements are unreasonable. Surely, somewhere, there hangs the all-purpose, collarless, sleeved, below-the-knee, flowing (but not too much), no-frills, flowerless, wrinkle-free garment of my dreams. I may have to widen my search area, but I shall continue my quest at least until Labor Day.

And if I'm not successful, there's always next summer, when boot camp fashion just might be all the rage!

About the Author

SUSAN GOLDFEIN is the author of *How Old Am I in Dog Years?* and *How to Complain When There's Nothing to Complain About,* which earned her multiple awards for humor writing.

She turned to writing as a second career, following her retirement as Doctor Susan, speech pathologist, professor, and consultant. As a staunch advocate for reinvention at any age, she vows to continue chronicling the third act of life with wisdom and wit, as long as she can remember where she left her glasses.

Her essays have appeared in *The Palm Beach Post* and Hearst Publications. She writes a monthly humor column for the online Florida publication *North Palm Beach Life,* a Nevada-based paper, *The Vegas Voice,* and is a syndicated columnist with other publications aimed at the senior market. She is the author of the blog *Susan's Unfiltered Wit, www.susansunfilteredwit.com.*

Hailing originally from New York, Susan currently lives in Florida with her husband, and their dog Sam, the world's cutest Russell Terrier.

THANK YOU FOR READING Susan Goldfein's *Laughing My Way Through the Third Stage*. If you enjoyed this book, here are some suggestions for sharing it:

- Write an online customer review wherever books are sold

- Gift this book to family and friends

- Share a photo of the book on social media and tag #SusanGoldfein and #LaughingMyWay3rdStage

- Bring in Susan Goldfein as a speaker for your club or organization

- Suggest *Laughing My Way* to your local book club

- For bulk order inquiries, contact Citrine Publishing at (828) 585-7030 or Publisher@CitrinePublishing.com

- Meet Susan Goldfein and read her latest essays at www.SusansUnfilteredWit.com

We appreciate your book reviews, letters and shares.

CITRINE PUBLISHING